My Impactful Life

NURISS CLARK

My Impactful Life

From pain to purpose

**Copyright © 2025 Nuriss Clark
All rights reserved.**

No part of this publication may be reproduced, stored in a retrieval system, or transmitted in any form or by any means—electronic, mechanical, photocopying, recording, or otherwise—without prior written permission from the copyright holder. This is a work of non-fiction based on real events. Some names and identifying details may have been changed to protect individuals' privacy.

ISBN: 979-8-9999448-3-2

For permissions or inquiries, please contact:
Nuriss Clark

Email: Nurisslife@gmail.com

DEDICATION

This book is dedicated to all those who have embarked on the journey of immigration, facing challenges, sacrifices, and loneliness in search of a better life.

To those who left behind their homeland and stumbled upon walls of indifference while trying to reach their dreams.

To the women who have been harassed or abused, and who fight to escape dangerous environments without knowing where to go.

To the homeless. To those without shelter, who each night search for a corner where they might sleep in peace.

To the children and young people who grow up without family, without guidance, without a safe embrace... I embrace you here, through these pages.

To all of you, I dedicate this book as a tribute to your strength and perseverance.

May God grant you soon a place of rest and peace—a home where you can feel protected, valued, and deeply loved.

And to every reader who has walked with me word by word:

May this story remind you that there is a God who sees, who listens, who restores, and who transforms.

Because if God did it for me... He can also do it for you.

ACKNOWLEDGMENTS

I want to begin this journey of gratitude by acknowledging God, my inexhaustible source of wisdom, strength, and guidance. Without His love and direction, this book would not have been possible. Every word written is infused with the certainty that it was He who gave me the courage, the strength, and the inspiration to move forward even in the midst of the hardest trials.

To my family and loved ones: Desirée, Laurie, Bradley, Lissette, and Angytto—thank you for your unconditional support, your patience, your love, and your faith in me. You have been the driving force that pushed me to keep going, even when the path seemed impossible.

To my friends and brothers and sisters at Alpha & Omega Church Miami, thank you for being a spiritual refuge in my life. Especially to Pastors Alberto and Mariam Delgado, for your leadership filled with wisdom, love, and vision. I bless you with all my heart.

To Pastors Gabriel and Ayskel Russian, who prophesied

that this book would reach the ends of the earth, and to Vicky Sotolongo, who also received a living word from God about this work. Thank you for reminding me of the eternal purpose behind every page.

I also thank Pastors Osorio, Minister Wellington, Ministers Maltez, and my friends from the "Bendecidos" group and the "Cumpleaños & Fiesta" group, who with their joy, prayers, and words of encouragement have uplifted my spirit in such a precious way.

My heartfelt thanks also go to:

Legna García, Madeline, Tito, Isabel, Blanca, Erika, John, María Luna, the Rollins family, Jacqueline, Zobeida, Lucesita, Pastor Griselda and family, Alexandria & Joey, Pablo, Gaby, Yngrith, Rosa, Yessika E, Cecilia Alegría, Fabio, Carolina, Denia, Zobeida, Lorena, María Peláez, Marina, Vivian, Ana, Milagros, Mirna, Paola, Vanessa, Yamil, Jimmy, Maribel, Odexsy, Yudeisy, Fer, Tatiana, Daira, Julio, Lilibeth, Débora, Aviaser, Ludyn, Alexa, María Luna, Kathya, Samon, Mary, Duber, Annette, Cadmiel, Johanna, María & Olga, Liliana, Hueimar, David, and to all my friends who have stood by my side. Your lives have touched mine in ways words can hardly describe.

This book is not only mine... it is also yours.
Thank you for walking with me.

LETTER TO THE READER

Thank you for opening the pages of this true testimony, born from the soul and forged in the most intense trials of life. Every chapter you will read is a sigh, a tear... and a victory.

This book is not only an autobiography; it is an open letter to broken hearts, a light for those who walk through dark paths, and an embrace for those who feel that no one understands them.

In these pages, I share my story just as it was lived: without adornments, without masks. I slept on trains. I cried in silence. I walked aimlessly with a shattered soul. But I also learned to rise, to believe in God's promises, and to discover that—even in the deepest valley—He is still at work.

This book is for you...

For you who have suffered.

For you who once thought of giving up.

For you who need to remember that you are not alone.

Thank you for allowing me to

walk with you through these pages.

Thank you for reading me with an open heart.

And above all, thank you for believing—as I once did—that out of pain, purpose is also born.

TABLE OF CONTENTS

Introduction 15
Chapter 1: Something Is About to Begin 17
Chapter 2: Where It All Began 23
Chapter 3: A Decision That Split the Path 35
Chapter 4: Obstacles, Farewell to Santo Domingo 85
Chapter 5: Arrival in the United States – First Steps 109
Chapter 6: When Everything Became Clouded 159
Chapter 7: Puerto Rico The Process That Shaped My Character 231
Chapter 8: The Refuge That Healed My Wounds 293
Chapter 9: Facing the Pain and Taking the First Step 311
Chapter 10: Agustín and the Promise of Home 329
Chapter 11: Driving Towards Purpose 361
Chapter 12: The Key to a Dream 387
Chapter 13: Conquered Territory 401
Conclusion: Up to Here... But Not the End 413
Final Prayer 419

INTRODUCTION

When I began writing this story, I did not do it from a place of comfort or success, but from the living memory of pain.

Each word was born in the crucible of struggle, in the echo of cold nights, in the trembling steps of walking alone through a country that was not my own.

This book is not merely a recounting of events. It is an emotional journey. It is a map of the soul of a teenage girl who, having no one, chose to believe. To believe in God. In His promises. In the possibility of tomorrow.

Through these pages you will relive not only my tears, but also the embraces I lacked, the nights I slept without a roof, the moments when I felt I would not make it... and the miracles that began to break through the pain.

Today, I welcome you to this story. To my story. But perhaps, also, to yours.

Because if you have ever felt unseen, if you have ever believed your voice didn't matter, or if you have thought the world has forgotten you... this book is for you. To remind you that yes, it is possible. That there is purpose behind the suffering. That God does not abandon.

Welcome, dear reader.
Thank you for being here.

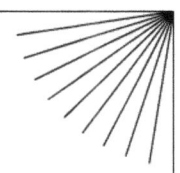

CHAPTER 1

Something Is About to Begin

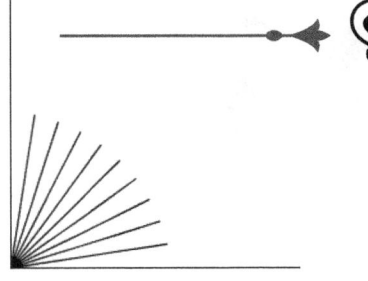

It was a fresh autumn morning. The playful wind swept the dry leaves across the ground, as if whispering a message only a few could understand.

In the distance, hurried footsteps echoed...

Tap, tap, tap!

Someone was running in haste, as if late to an appointment destiny had marked long ago.

Children's laughter rose through the hallways, bouncing off the walls and floating in the air like tiny bubbles of joy.

Meanwhile, pencils had already begun their dance across the paper.

Scratch, scratch, scratch...

The sound of graphite gliding filled the classroom like a soft murmur in the background.

Everything seemed the same as every morning...

But something was different.

A feeling.

An invisible whisper.

A premonition floating in the air.

The classroom door swung open.

"Hello, hello, hello!" greeted Ms. Grey, with her ever-radiant smile.

The children responded in chorus, cheerful, unaware of what was about to happen.

At that very moment, I stepped into the room.

At first, no one seemed to notice. But I felt it.

Deep within my chest, something tightened slightly.

A small inner voice whispered in my ear:

"This day will change everything."

The wind slipped through the window, stirring the curtains as if trying to announce the beginning of something important.

The children took their seats.

The pencils fell still.

The teacher grew silent.

And then...

A heavy silence wrapped the classroom.

It wasn't a silence to fear... but one that made the heart beat just a little faster.

As if the universe, in that instant, were about to unveil a secret.

And without yet understanding why...

I knew, with absolute certainty,

that nothing would ever be the same again.

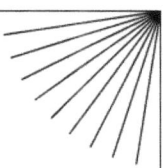

CHAPTER 2

Where It All Began: Childhood, Adolescence, Faith, Revelations, Dreams and the First Impulse

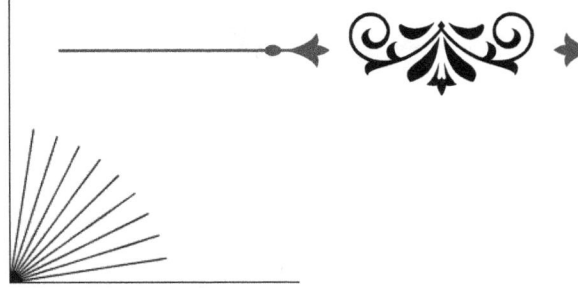

CHAPTER 2

Where It All Began:
Childhood, Adolescence, Faith,
Revelations, Dreams and
the First Impulse

I close my eyes... and immediately, I return.

I return to that time when faith filled everything.

When we had no luxuries, but something that shone brighter than any treasure:

the presence of God in our home.

My mother would rise each day before the sun.

There was no alarm clock, no breakfast served yet.

What woke us was something far more powerful: prayer.

Her soft voice traveled through every corner, as if God Himself walked through our home in the dim light of dawn.

And while the world outside still slept, within our house invisible battles were already being fought... on our knees.

My father was a humble pastor at the Assembly of God Church.

I never saw him complain, nor be filled with pride.

I only saw him with a Bible in his hand and a faith that would not bend.

I remember the hymns:

"I will praise, I will praise, I will praise my Lord…"

That melody was tattooed on my soul; it became part of the foundations of my heart.

Before I knew how to read, I could already recite psalms.

Before I learned the alphabet, I already knew how to talk to God.

We lived with little, but we had much.

We were seven siblings. We shared the material things, but the most valuable was invisible:

values.

Our house was simple, but it was full of something unseen:

presence, purpose, and protection.

My parents were the pillars. They didn't need elaborate words; their surrendered lives spoke louder than anything else.

They taught us that if we trusted in God, He would always be our refuge.

And that became the foundation of everything.

I grew up among emotions, struggles, and lessons.

At first, I studied at a little school in my hometown: Sánchez, Samaná, near Las Terrenas.

There, I met Miss Grey.

And without me knowing it... she saw something in me.

Something different.

"This girl doesn't belong in the first grade," she once said.

They tested me and, to everyone's surprise, I was placed in the third grade.

The same teacher who had discovered me was left speechless.

From that moment, I knew something profound:

I can move forward, even when the world says, *"wait."*

After some time, we moved to Santo Domingo.

I studied at Montessori School, where once again I was promoted, this time to sixth grade.

Then, life took us to Piedra Blanca de Bonao.

At the Ambrosia Ramírez de Abad School, I was enrolled

in sixth grade, but soon after, they moved me up to eighth. It wasn't easy. But I learned a lesson that has stayed with me always:

What God plants in your mind, no one can stop.

The faith that had been planted in me was not just religion. It was fire.

It was what kept me dreaming, even when our pockets were empty.

And when we returned to Sánchez, that fire burned even stronger.

Our Pentecostal church was a whirlwind of living faith.

And in the middle of that revival, something unexpected happened:

I, still a child, would stand at the front and preach.

The words didn't come from me… They flowed.

People shouted: *"Amen!" "Hallelujah!"*

I only felt that I was speaking what God placed in my heart.

I remember the astonished faces. Older people with tears. Others with smiles.

MY IMPACTFUL LIFE: FROM PAIN TO PURPOSE

And me... simply speaking, my heart pounding fast.

But not everything was easy.

I began to have dreams... Different dreams. I would see things that were going to happen. Sometimes, even the death of close relatives. I told my parents. They listened with respect and attention.

They knew something special was happening to me.

But I was just a child... And though I felt I had a gift, it scared me. Slowly, I began to silence that spiritual side... Maybe out of fear, maybe because I didn't know what to do with so much.

Today, I ask myself: *What if I had embraced it from the beginning?*

Perhaps... many things in my life would have been different.

At twelve years old, my life changed completely.

One night, I felt it. God spoke to me clearly, as if calling me by name.

He showed me that my path would not be easy... but that it carried an eternal purpose.

And so my journey began.

A journey filled with trials, tears, and miracles.

A journey where faith would be my shield.

And where every fall would be part of the plan to rise stronger.

A Teenage Girl with Wings and Wounds

I was only twelve years old... but inside, I felt as if the world was already demanding that I become an adult.

On the outside, I was still a child.

On the inside, a silent war was beginning to burn.

After that moment when I felt God spoke to me so clearly, everything changed.

I was no longer just the little girl who recited psalms.

Now I had questions...

Feelings I didn't understand...

Dreams that hurt...

And a faith that was still alive, but that began to tremble with the confusing winds of adolescence.

My parents remained my anchor.

Yet I felt that something in me was starting to loosen.

As if my wings wanted to fly...

but the sky was heavy with storms.

At school, I no longer felt like I belonged anywhere.

I was the one who advanced faster, the one who thought differently, the one who didn't fit in.

And though many looked at me with admiration for my achievements,

all I wanted was to be a normal girl.

I began to feel lonely.

Not because I lacked people around me...

but because no one understood what was happening inside me.

The nights became my refuge.

There, between the sheets and my silent tears, I would speak to God.

I told Him about my fears.

I asked Him why I felt this way.

And even though I often received no answers...

I felt that He was listening.

It was also during that stage that the world showed its harsh face.

Things began to change at home.

Financial struggles grew tighter.

Arguments became more frequent.

And although Mom and Dad kept fighting with faith, the atmosphere was no longer the same.

I, who had come from such a protected childhood,

began to understand that life also hits hard.

And that the most difficult was yet to come...

One day, without warning, life shook us to the core.

We had to pack everything and move.

Again. It was like starting over, only this time with more fear and less hope.

I left behind my school, my friends, my church.

MY IMPACTFUL LIFE: FROM PAIN TO PURPOSE

And though my faith was still alive, it felt wounded.

In that new place, everything was different.

Different people. Harsh looks. A cold environment.

And there I was:

a teenage girl with a heart full of faith,

with a soul full of questions.

Where are You, God?

Why do I feel so alone?

Do I really have a purpose?

And it was in the middle of that darkness… that I began to write.

I didn't know those words would become part of my healing.

I wrote prayers.

Verses that calmed me.

Dreams I didn't understand.

And promises I held onto.

My notebook became my secret hiding place.

There, I could be myself.

There, no one judged me.

There, I felt that even though the world wasn't listening…

God was.

My adolescence was a mixture of struggles, of lights and of shadows.

I learned to fake smiles.

To carry pain in silence.

To be strong, even when inside I felt shattered.

But something within me—something that never died—

kept whispering that all of this had a purpose.

And that voice… that voice I heard when I was a child… kept telling me:

"Do not give up.

You haven't yet seen what I am going to do with you."

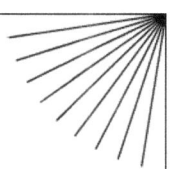

CHAPTER 3

A Decision That Split the Path – Passport, Visa to Greece, American Consulate

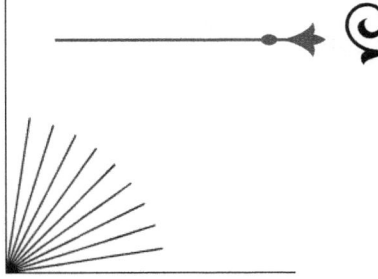

After so many changes, life once again took us back to the capital. We returned to Santo Domingo.

Everything seemed to move quickly, as if decisions would not wait for the heart to be ready.

One day, without much explanation, my mother looked me straight in the eyes.

In her gaze there was affection, but also determination.

"You're going to stay with your grandparents," she told me, trying to sound firm.

My heart skipped a beat.

I didn't immediately understand what that meant.

Yet somehow, without anyone saying it, I knew my life was about to change again.

My parents needed to return to La Hormiga, a small neighborhood near Las Terrenas in Sánchez, Samaná. There, their calling awaited them.

My father was a pastor of the Assembly of God Church, and his duty to God always came first. I knew how much he loved his ministry.

I had seen him preach with passion, serve tirelessly, and weep in prayer for others.

And though I understood his devotion, a part of me quietly broke inside.

My grandparents, Pedro Pablo and Emilia, welcomed me with love.

They were noble people, the kind who always had a cup of coffee ready and wise advice at the tip of their tongue.

But inside... I felt alone.

It wasn't my home.

It wasn't my room.

It wasn't my immediate family.

It was like being on pause, as if life had stopped only for me, while everyone else kept moving forward.

The nights were the hardest.

I would lie in bed staring at the ceiling, my soul filled with questions:

Why did they leave me here?

Why couldn't they take me with them?

God, are You seeing this?

I clung to the psalms my mother had taught me,

to the promises I once heard.

But the silence hurt.

Every time I heard my father's or mother's name, a mix of pride and sorrow tightened my chest.

I knew my father was doing the right thing, serving God… but all I wanted was his embrace.

And there, in that quiet house—between the slow footsteps of my grandparents and the days that seemed to repeat themselves—another stage of life began.

A stage that taught me to grow inwardly.

To listen to God in the silence.

To find strength where there was none.

I didn't know then that all of this was preparing me.

I didn't know that very soon my life would take a turn that would change everything.

A turn that would take me far.

Very far.

My grandparents' house was simple, but it carried something special:

the smell of freshly brewed coffee,

of clean clothes drying under the sun,

and of prayers that seemed never to end.

My brother Julián lived there too.

Having him close was like a ray of sunshine in the middle of so much confusion.

We were very different, yet there was a bond between us that couldn't be broken.

He was quieter, more reserved.

His presence gave me peace.

Sometimes I would sit next to him without saying a word.

Just being near him helped me not think so much about what I had left behind.

Things felt more bearable when Julián was around.

The days passed slowly.

Between school, house chores, and prayers with my grandparents, time seemed to stretch endlessly.

I tried to be strong, I tried to smile...

But inside, I felt something was missing.

I missed my parents.

I missed my church.

I missed feeling like I belonged somewhere.

And though my grandparents were loving, there was always this constant feeling of being "in transit," as if my soul already knew this wasn't my final destination.

Something inside me told me that all this was just preparation.

Julián would sometimes see me sad and say:

"Everything will be alright, Nuriss. You are strong. God has something great for you."

I wanted to believe him.

And maybe, deep down, I did.

But there were also moments when my faith wavered.

The nights remained long.

And many times I cried in silence, clutching my pillow,

remembering the dreams I had as a child,

the times I preached in church,

the words I felt God had spoken to me.

I wondered if all of that had been real...

or just part of my childish imagination.

But then something would happen.

A sensation, a thought, a whisper in my soul...

telling me:

"The real beginning has not yet come."

And that phrase stayed with me like a promise.

Like a seed beginning to grow in secret.

Because though I didn't know it yet...

my life was about to change forever.

The Announcement That Awakened a Dream

One ordinary afternoon, the sun filtered through the wooden slats of my grandmother's house.

The air smelled of freshly brewed coffee and damp earth.

I was sitting in the rocking chair on the porch, flipping through the newspaper my grandfather bought every day—more out of habit than interest—and left on the table.

The pages crackled with each movement, while the world seemed to move at a slower rhythm in that little corner of Santo Domingo.

And then I saw it.

An announcement in bold letters, as if leaping off the page to catch me:

"SCHOLARSHIPS TO GREECE!"

My heart skipped a beat.

I leaned forward, read it again, making sure my eyes weren't deceiving me.

"Scholarships… to Greece?" I whispered.

A current of electricity ran through my body.

I imagined the ruins of the Parthenon, the ancient temples, the thousand-year-old statues… Athens!

I, a teenage girl with big dreams, walking down those very streets, breathing in that history.

"This is for me!" I told myself. "I'm smart, I can win that scholarship."

In my mind I pictured myself boarding a plane, traveling to the other side of the world, exploring ancient lands, as if everything I had lived up to that moment had only been a prelude to something much greater.

But suddenly, my excitement came to a halt when I read the requirements:

"Scholarships available only for archaeology students."

And I was not an archaeology student.

My chest tightened.

I felt that mix of disappointment and anger, like when you see a door half-open, but as you approach, you realize it's locked.

But I did not give up.

Something inside me clung to that dream.

I decided, without knowing how or when, that I was going to leave.

To Greece or wherever God willed—but I was going.

It was a deep certainty, impossible to ignore.

I didn't have the means, the support, not even a plan…

but in my spirit, I had already taken the first step.

And without knowing it yet,

that was the very moment when God's plan was set in motion.

God's Calling Over My Life

Days after having seen that scholarship announcement to Greece, my mind could not stop dreaming of other destinations.

Even though I knew those scholarships were not for me, something had been awakened deep within me.

It was as if heaven had opened an invisible door, stirring inside me an uncontrollable desire to leave, to search for my purpose beyond familiar borders.

One night, while everyone slept and silence reigned in the house, I lay down staring at the wooden ceiling, my heart restless. I closed my eyes and prayed silently.

I spoke to God as a daughter speaks to her Father about her deepest longings, with no filter and no shame.

And then it happened. I could not explain it in human words, but it was as if time stood still.

A supernatural peace surrounded me.

And there, in the stillness of the night, I heard His voice:

—*No. You will not go to Greece.*

—*I want you in the United States.*

MY IMPACTFUL LIFE: FROM PAIN TO PURPOSE

My body trembled.

I sat up in bed, breathless.

"How am I going to do that, Lord?" I whispered, my heart racing.

"How can I go to the United States when it requires a visa, permission, and documents?"

The answer came without delay. It wasn't reasoning.

It was a deep certainty.

—*I will show you what you must do.*

My eyes filled with tears.

It was God Himself speaking to me.

It was not imagination. It was not mere emotion.

It was His voice... as real as the sound of rain striking the roof.

That night, I could not sleep.

I stayed awake praying, crying, asking... believing.

A new faith—strong and alive—was born within me.

I didn't understand the path, but I knew I had direction.

And I was not alone.

From that moment on, everything changed.

I was no longer just a girl with vague dreams.

Now I was a young woman with a calling from the Lord.

When God speaks, the heavens open, doors align,

and the impossible becomes a path.

I knew trials would come. I knew it would not be easy.

But one thing was certain: my journey to the United States had already begun... in the spirit.

My restlessness had not gone unnoticed by heaven.

That whisper inside me was not just an echo in my soul,

it was the beginning of a sacred conversation.

And when I asked again, with fear and faith intertwined:

"How will I do it, Lord? How will I fulfill this impossible calling?"

The answer descended like a balm:

—*I will show you what you must do. Just wait for My instructions.*

It was then that I understood it was not about my strength, nor my intelligence, nor my resources.

What was about to happen did not depend on me, but on God.

And in that instant, I surrendered completely to a journey of faith, of obedience, and of total dependence on the Lord.

That very night, while the world slept and silence covered everything, I fell into a deep sleep—one unlike any I had ever had before.

It was not an ordinary dream.

It was a visitation from heaven. A revelation.

In the dream, I saw myself walking toward an unfamiliar city.

The streets were new to me. Yet there was something familiar in the air: peace, overwhelming peace.

Suddenly, I saw a great white door, and in front of it, a voice told me:

—First go to the Greek consulate. Do not ask why. Just obey. I will open doors there.

I awoke startled. My heart pounded—not with fear, but with a heavenly excitement.

A clear and direct instruction had been given.

And even though I did not understand why Greece if the final destination was the United States, I knew I had to obey.

God does not always reveal the entire path.

Sometimes, He only gives us the first step.

And that first step... I already had.

That morning, I rose with a different determination.

The girl full of doubts had been left behind.

Now I was a young woman chosen, guided by the voice of the Almighty.

And though I had no documents, no money, no human connections...

I had a word.

A word from God that was more than enough to move mountains.

A Revelation That Would Change My Destiny

The next morning, as the first rays of sunlight barely peeked through, I rose with my heart racing. The experience of the previous night still burned within me like a flame that would not go out. I could still clearly hear that gentle yet firm voice that had spoken to me in my dream... the voice of God.

He had told me something that defied logic, yet resonated as absolute truth deep within my soul:

— I will take you to the United States. I Myself will show you the way.

How could I keep something so sacred only to myself? I knew I had to share it with my family, even though my heart trembled at the thought that they might not believe me.

It was a message from the Lord that deserved to be revealed with reverence.

That dream was not a simple reflection of human desires; it was a divine revelation. And as such, it had to be shared.

My heart pounded as I walked toward the kitchen, a whirlwind stirring inside me. I had clearly heard God's voice—the same voice that had accompanied me in so many stages of my life—and now it gave me an instruction that seemed impossible: to go to the United States. That is why I felt the need to tell my family.

I could not keep something so great, so sacred, only to myself.

I had to communicate what the Lord had revealed to me, even though I knew it would not be easy.

My mother was in the kitchen, the smell of coffee filling the air while the birdsong marked the beginning of what seemed like an ordinary day. But for me, nothing would ever be the same again.

I approached, trembling yet brave.

"Mami, Papi... I need to tell you something," I stammered, trying to keep my voice steady though my emotions threatened to overflow.

My siblings began to gather around, one by one, as if the Holy Spirit were calling them too. We sat in the living room. I took a deep breath, closed my eyes for a moment, and spoke.

"Last night I had a dream, but it wasn't just any dream. I heard the voice of the Lord. He spoke to me clearly. He told me that He would take me to the United States. And that He would show me what I must do there."

MY IMPACTFUL LIFE: FROM PAIN TO PURPOSE

A deep silence fell.

My mother looked at me intently. There was tenderness on her face, and also a special brightness in her eyes, as if she recognized that what I was saying came from above. She had heard many times that God speaks through dreams, but hearing this from her own daughter left her speechless.

"And what did He say, my daughter? Are you sure of what you're saying?" she asked softly.

In that moment, I didn't have all the answers, but I had certainty.

What I felt in that dream was not imagination, nor a fleeting desire.

It was a deep conviction, a supernatural peace that left no room for doubt.

I swallowed hard. My hands trembled slightly.

"Yes, Mami," I replied, tears welling up. "God confirmed it to me. I know it sounds crazy, but I am not alone. He is with me."

It was not imagination.

It was not desire.

It was conviction.

A supernatural peace had taken hold of me.

My father, who until then had remained silent, lowered his gaze. His strong hands intertwined. Then he lifted his eyes and said:

"If it was God who spoke to you… I would not dare to stop what He has begun. Just walk in faith."

In that moment, I felt that the Lord had not only spoken to me. He was also touching their hearts.

My sister Carmen Juana stood up, hugged me tightly, and whispered in my ear:

"If God is sending you, don't think twice. He will open doors. And I will be with you too."

Then, like a wave of divine love, each of my siblings began to respond.

Rosa Chovy, always so curious, wanted to know the details.

Lourdes didn't say much, but just by looking at me I knew her heart had also believed.

Julián was astonished and couldn't take his eyes off me.

And María Belkis, with her wide, amazed eyes, seemed to see in me the reflection of something sacred.

That day, the entire house was filled with something different.

It was not fear.

It was not doubt.

It was a sense of purpose, of calling.

Later, my father took my hand and told me something that would mark my spirit forever:

"If God said it... God will do it."

That day, the heavenly promise ceased to be a private whisper.

It became a shared declaration.

A step of faith that I would no longer take alone.

My family was walking with me.

And heaven—yes, heaven—had already begun to open.

The Passport of Purpose

The days passed between the routine at my grandparents' house and my own thoughts, which grew deeper with each moment.

I had received a clear message from God…

but I did not understand how it was going to be fulfilled.

The only thing I carried in my heart were those two words:

"United States."

And then, just when I thought nothing would move forward soon, my father arrived.

He returned to the capital, Santo Domingo, from his church in Samaná.

He appeared with his calm walk, his serene face, and that gaze that always brought both peace and firmness.

He didn't bring gifts.

He didn't bring promises.

He only brought a decision:

—*We're going to get you a passport.*

MY IMPACTFUL LIFE: FROM PAIN TO PURPOSE

My heart leapt.

I hadn't expected it.

But I knew that was the next step.

The step that would open the door to the purpose God had shown me.

We rose early.

The sun was just beginning to paint the city rooftops in orange.

As we walked together toward the passport office, I felt something special.

It wasn't just paperwork...

It was a sign.

My father was believing in me.

He was responding, perhaps without even knowing it, to the plan God had already set in motion.

He didn't ask many questions.

He simply walked beside me, as if he knew this was something he had to do.

I remember the endless line, the forms, the eternal wait.

I could barely stay still.

I was afraid.

I was excited.

I felt everything all at once inside my chest.

When our turn came, we handed over the documents.

"Is she a minor?" the clerk asked.

"Yes, but she's going to travel," my father said firmly, as one who declares something already real.

He signed the papers.

He looked at me with a mix of pride… and farewell.

And in that instant, I understood everything:

My father was entrusting me.

Not only to a country…

but to a purpose.

When they finally handed me the passport, I held it in my hands as if it were a treasure.

It was small.

It was red.

But inside, it carried a destiny I could not even imagine.

We left in silence.

I wanted to hug him.

To tell him how much that meant to me.

But I stayed quiet, just looking at him as we walked.

And I think he knew.

He placed his hand on my shoulder, as he often did, and said:

"Trust. What God begins, He will finish."

I didn't know when the journey would happen.

I didn't know how, or with what resources.

But I already had the passport.

And that, for me, was the confirmation that heaven had already begun moving its pieces.

The next step would be to obey…

And to wait for the divine instruction I knew would come very soon.

The Visa to Greece

Sometimes God gives you instructions that don't seem to make sense…

Yet every step, no matter how strange it may appear, is perfectly calculated by Him.

The announcement about the scholarships to Greece kept circling in my mind.

It was in a dream that the Lord spoke to me again.

I was on my knees, as I was every night, praying in silence.

And as I slept, I felt it.

That voice I already knew.

Calm, firm, unwavering.

It was the voice of the Lord.

—*Go to the Greek consulate. Get the visa.*

I woke up confused.

Greece, Lord? Wasn't it that You wanted me in the United States?

But I received no further answers.

Only that clear command engraved in my mind when I awoke:

—*Go to the Greek consulate.*

And I obeyed.

A few days later, I went alone to the Greek consulate.

I didn't know why God was asking me to do this.

But I trusted that He knew more than I did.

Me... a teenage girl with no resources, no contacts, no companions.

But with determination.

The place was small.

There were few people, no pressure.

And to my surprise, the process was quick.

The questions were basic.

And before I realized it, they handed me the visa with a smile:

"Congratulations. Your visa is approved."

I was in shock.

Really?

I had in my hands a visa to Greece.

A faraway, unknown country.

But real.

I left the consulate with my mind confused and my heart divided, pounding hard.

Not with excitement...

but with bewilderment.

Is this what God wants? Could Greece be my destiny after all?

I had the visa.

I held it in my hands.

But something didn't feel right.

It wasn't peace that I felt.

MY IMPACTFUL LIFE: FROM PAIN TO PURPOSE

It was a burning question:

Why did You send me here, Lord?

That night, as I slept with the Greek visa tucked in my nightstand,

the voice returned.

But this time... it was more direct.

—*No. You will not go to Greece.*

I remained still, half-asleep yet listening.

—*I want you in the United States. But you had to obtain that visa first. Trust Me.*

My soul trembled.

The dream felt more real than the day itself.

—*Now go to the American consulate.*

—*But Lord, what about the Greek visa? What was the purpose of all this?*

—*Obey. I will show you.*

I awoke shaken, my heart beating like a drum.

I could still feel His presence in the room.

And I knew...

I knew with absolute certainty...

that Greece was not my destiny.

It was a test of obedience.

A preparation.

A necessary step, though not the final one.

God had led me to that consulate not to travel,

but to teach me that His voice stands above logic.

That if I could obey what I didn't understand,

I could also trust in what I could not yet see.

That the "right" thing is not always the most obvious.

And that obedience sometimes means letting go of what is already in your hands... for something you cannot see yet.

I broke down in tears.

Not of sadness,

but of reverence.

MY IMPACTFUL LIFE: FROM PAIN TO PURPOSE

I understood that if a visa had been granted to me so easily...

it was only to prove one thing:

My faithfulness.

Would I follow my own desires?

Or would I follow God's instruction?

My answer was only one:

—*I will obey.*

And so, with the visa to Greece still fresh in my hands...

I prepared to present myself at the American consulate.

With no guarantee.

With no logical reason.

But with the certainty that heaven had already decided for me.

That was how, with an approved visa to Greece...

and a burning calling to the United States...

I prepared to go to the American consulate.

This time, with a heart more surrendered than ever.

Knowing that each step was directed from heaven...

even if I did not yet understand why.

The American Consulate and the Voice of Heaven

After obtaining the passport and a visa to Greece, something in me changed.

It was no longer just a vision.

It was no longer just a dream.

Now there was a door slightly open...

and I only needed the courage to push it.

Although I still didn't know how it would happen,

I knew I was going.

The words of the Lord kept echoing within me, like a gentle but insistent whisper:

"Just wait for My instructions."

Days passed, and one night, like so many others, I knelt beside my bed.

I closed my eyes, but my heart was restless.

I wanted to understand. I wanted to know the next step.

I lay down to sleep and, in the middle of the night,

the voice returned.

Clear. Calm. Impossible to ignore:

—*Now go to the American consulate.*

I opened my eyes wide.

I stayed still.

I didn't need further explanations.

I knew what I had to do.

The next morning, I rose before dawn.

The sky was only beginning to lighten.

It was very early, but I was already dressed, ready, and determined.

I had no one to accompany me.

I had no extra money nor the certainty that I would be approved.

But I had a promise from God... and that was enough.

I went out alone.

The morning air hit my face, but I didn't feel cold.

I felt purpose.

When I arrived at the consulate, the line was already long.

Well-dressed adults with folders full of documents.

They all looked confident, prepared, accompanied.

I only had my passport... and an unshakable faith.

There I was, in silence.

I looked at everyone, but inside, I spoke to God:

"I am here, Lord. Do not let me go. Do not leave me alone."

The hours passed slowly.

The sun was already high when I finally crossed the doors of the consulate.

Inside, the atmosphere was tense.

MY IMPACTFUL LIFE: FROM PAIN TO PURPOSE

The air conditioning was freezing.

The white lights, too bright.

The murmurs, barely audible.

No one smiled.

In front of me, a line of people waited their turn.

Each with their folder perfectly organized, their papers in order, their answers rehearsed.

I only had my passport… my faith… and trembling legs.

I looked toward the windows.

And there she was.

The consul.

The same one I had seen reject applicant after applicant:

"I'm sorry. You do not qualify."

"I'm sorry. You do not qualify."

"I'm sorry. You do not qualify."

One after another, broken dreams in front of me.

Some cried.

Others argued.

It was as if hopes were being shattered right before my eyes.

Everything inside me screamed that I had no chance.

I was only a teenage girl.

Alone.

Without backing.

Without any strong document to qualify me.

And yet...

there I was.

With every step the line advanced, my heart beat louder:

Thump... Thump... Thump...

I felt my knees weaken.

I wanted to run.

I wanted to hide.

But then I remembered:

"Do not be afraid, I am with you."

The words of the Lord returned like a warm whisper covering my chest.

Something inside me trembled.

But it wasn't fear.

It was His presence.

"Trust," my soul whispered.

I closed my eyes.

And I began to pray.

In a low voice, as if raising an invisible wall around me, I recited my favorite psalms:

"He who dwells in the shelter of the Most High

Will rest in the shadow of the Almighty.

I will say of the Lord, 'He is my refuge and my fortress,

My God, in whom I trust.'" (Psalm 91:1–2)

"The Lord is my shepherd, I lack nothing.

Even though I walk through the darkest valley,

I will fear no evil, for You are with me..." (Psalm 23:1, 4)

"I lift up my eyes to the mountains—

Where does my help come from?

My help comes from the Lord,

The Maker of heaven and earth." (Psalm 121:1–2)

Again and again.

Each word was a solid rock beneath my feet.

Each verse, an invisible shield around me.

When I opened my eyes, there were only two people left before me.

And the consul kept rejecting:

"I'm sorry. You do not qualify."

I swallowed hard.

My stomach churned.

My hands gripped the passport tightly.

And then...

My name.

Everything stopped.

MY IMPACTFUL LIFE: FROM PAIN TO PURPOSE

The noise faded.

My feet walked on their own toward the window.

The consul looked at me.

Her penetrating gaze, as if she wanted to read my soul.

And then she asked:

—"What part of the United States are you going to?"

For a second, no words came out.

But I remembered:

"Obey."

I took a deep breath.

"To Miami," I replied, with all the firmness I could gather.

One second.

Two.

Silence.

A flicker of doubt crossed her face…

And then, it happened.

She smiled.

Her voice, once harsh like a sentence, now warm:

—"Have a good trip. Welcome to the United States."

She handed me the passport with the visa.

My hands trembled.

My eyes filled with tears.

I didn't know whether to shout, laugh, or fall to my knees.

But the only words that came out of my lips were:

"Glory to God!" I said out loud, unashamed.

God had done it.

A teenage girl. Alone. Without money. Without property. Without company.

But with a word in her heart… and the backing of heaven.

In that moment, I knew, more clearly than ever:

God opens doors that no one can shut.

And that consulate, which had seemed like an impossible wall…

became the first victory in my journey toward the extraordinary.

I still did not know all that was to come.

But that day, my journey into the unpredictable began.

The Breaking News of a Miracle

My words of gratitude echoed through the consulate office like a cry of victory:

"Glory to God!" I exclaimed, tears in my eyes.

I didn't care who was watching.

I didn't care if they understood.

He had done it.

A teenage girl—without possessions, without supporting documents, without a companion—had obtained an American visa solely by God's command.

I left there rejoicing with overflowing joy for what I had just experienced.

I felt as if I were floating, as if the ground no longer held me.

But I also knew something:

this was only the beginning.

When I arrived home, the news was received as a true miracle.

My grandparents could not believe it.

My sister Carmen Juana and my brother Julián looked at me with silent pride.

My whole family was left speechless, all in awe.

And my mother? ...Though she smiled, her mind was already moving to what would come next:

"Now we need to get the ticket."

But we had no way.

There were no savings.

No bank accounts.

No relatives who could help us.

I kept my passport like a treasure.

Carefully tucked inside an envelope,

it became the physical evidence of a blind and total faith.

The house filled with a strange mixture:

joy, disbelief, and silence.

Everyone knew it was a miracle.

Everyone celebrated.

But I... I knew something more: this was only the beginning.

Because although God had opened that door,

He had also whispered to the depths of my soul:

"Prepare yourself. Greater trials still await you."

And I could not imagine what awaited me.

I only had certainty of one thing:

He would not let me go.

The Light Before the Flight

The sun was setting slowly that afternoon, as if it knew something sacred was taking place.

The sky, painted in shades of orange and gold, seemed like a heavenly sigh, as if God Himself were drawing a sign over Santo Domingo.

I was at home, sitting with my heart beating harder than usual.

In my trembling hands I held the U.S. visa.

It was not just a piece of paper.

It was a promise.

A key.

A direct answer from heaven to my prayers.

I had no property.

No riches.

No one to stand with me at the consulate window.

But heaven had said yes.

That miracle could not be explained by logic.

It was God, and only God, who had opened that impossible door.

I was excited. While people slept or went about their daily tasks,

I was living a moment that would change my life forever.

MY IMPACTFUL LIFE: FROM PAIN TO PURPOSE

Grateful.

But also... full of fear.

Because although the visa was in my hands, the question was another:

And now what?

I had no relatives in the United States.

No place to arrive.

Not even the plane ticket.

And the clock did not stop.

Fear crept through the cracks of my mind:

What if I don't make it there?

What if they send me back?

What if I end up like many who left and returned empty-handed?

I had heard stories of people who crossed the ocean in search of opportunities

and returned in debt and disappointment.

The future was uncertain.

But right in the middle of those questions, a light appeared: hope.

Not just any hope.

It was a hope planted by God, telling me:

"I am sending you. I will sustain you."

And then, that mixture of fear and faith began to transform into something new: conviction.

My mother, seeing everything that was happening, knew we had to act quickly.

There was no money.

No hidden savings.

But she…

that woman of faith, silent warrior, tireless in love,

decided to do something only a mother could do:

She sold the stove.

Our only stove.

The one that heated the beans.

The one that cooked the rice every day.

The heart of our kitchen.

Witness of so many family nights.

It became the ticket to my destiny.

For her, my calling was more important than any pot or fire.

And that stove became my passage.

Literally.

With that money, she bought my one-way ticket to the United States.

The sale covered just enough for a one-way fare.

The return was not even an option.

There was no return.

Only faith.

When we finally held the ticket in hand, our home was filled with a special joy.

The news spread through the family, the neighbors, and the church.

Everyone celebrated.

Everyone knew it was not something ordinary.

"They gave that girl an American visa!" people said in amazement.

But I knew the truth:

It was a miracle.

The hugs, the tears, the congratulations filled the air.

But inside, I was silent.

Not from sadness, but from reverence.

Because I knew I was about to leave everything behind.

That night, while the noise calmed and everyone returned to their routines,

I sat alone.

I looked at my passport.

I touched the envelope with the ticket.

And I looked up to the sky.

I knew this was not just a trip.

MY IMPACTFUL LIFE: FROM PAIN TO PURPOSE

It was a mission.

And though I had no idea what awaited me,

a certainty covered me like a mantle:

"God chose me. And He will go with me."

What no one knew was that, just before traveling,

my life was in danger.

An unexpected episode—dark and threatening—

almost shattered all the plans.

But it didn't.

Because when God has said *"You will go,"*

there is no hell that can say *"No."*

And that chapter...

I will also tell.

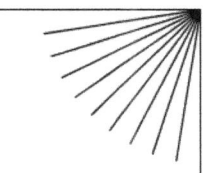

CHAPTER 4

Obstacles, Farewell to Santo Domingo and Flight to Miami

That Sunday began like any other.

The sky was clear, the breeze was gentle,

and the birdsong seemed to announce peace.

But inside me, a storm was raging.

My heart was restless.

The trip to the United States was approaching, and although I already had the visa in hand,

an invisible knot tightened in my chest:

fear, anxiety, doubts.

I didn't understand why, but something told me that day would not be ordinary.

Seeking comfort, I decided to spend the day at my sister Zunilda's house.

The church was near her home.

I wanted to go to church, to sing, to pray, to calm my spirit.

As soon as I arrived, her voice stopped me like a wall:

"No, you can't go out today. I have to leave, and José will send someone to pick up some tools. Stay in the house."

Something in her look was urgent.

I didn't argue.

I resigned myself, not knowing I was about to live one of the most terrifying moments of my life.

Around 10:30 a.m., someone knocked on the door.

It was a man. In his thirties. A stranger.

His face meant nothing to me.

"I came for the tools. José sent me, and he wants you to come with me."

My body tensed.

Everything inside me screamed:

Don't go!

I told him no.

I repeated that I wasn't going anywhere with him.

But he insisted.

And he pushed me.

He forced me out into the street.

Made me walk with him.

In my mind, I still wanted to believe something had happened to my sister,

and that this man was taking me to help her.

But everything felt wrong.

We got into a shared taxi, one of those "carros de concho" as they call them in Santo Domingo.

I sat silently.

My breathing quickened.

My heart pounded in my chest like a frantic drum.

Where is he taking me? Why did he push me? What is happening?

We entered the Sánchez highway.

Mile after mile.

The man's silence was more terrifying than any words.

Finally, we stopped in a deserted place.

No houses, no shops, no people.

Only weeds, dust, and an old house hidden among the brush.

My skin bristled.

Everything inside me screamed:

Run! This isn't right!

"Let's go," he ordered. "Get inside."

"No! I don't want to! I'm not going in!" I shouted.

I resisted.

I cried.

His eyes were empty.

Cold.

And then I knew:

I was in danger. Real danger.

Fear paralyzed me for an instant...

but something stronger pushed me to act.

I ran.

MY IMPACTFUL LIFE: FROM PAIN TO PURPOSE

I ran as if my life were escaping with each stride.

I ran as if the wind itself carried me.

And he, behind me.

A huge fence of iron and aluminum loomed in front of me.

There was no way out.

It was impossible to cross.

But then... the miracle happened.

I felt as though an invisible force lifted me.

As if giant hands had raised me from the ground

and thrown me through the air.

I don't remember how I did it.

I only know that, in the blink of an eye,

I was already on the other side.

Unharmed.

Free.

But with legs and feet scraped and bleeding.

The people who came near couldn't believe it.

They all said the same thing:

"That girl flew! God saved her!"

I couldn't speak.

I just cried.

I cried because I had seen death...

and God's hand had saved me from it.

People surrounded me and then took me back to my sister's house.

I returned to Zunilda's home as if coming back from a battle.

When she saw me, she broke down in tears.

She couldn't stop hugging me.

She looked at me with terror... but also with gratitude:

"God saved you, my sister. He saved you..." she repeated over and over.

That night I couldn't sleep.

I lay down with my soul shaken,

but with my faith stronger than ever.

I no longer had doubts.

I no longer asked why.

I knew the enemy wanted to stop my journey.

Wanted to break God's plans.

But he couldn't.

Because when heaven decides you will go…

no one can stop it.

My wounds were small.

But the message was profound.

God had rescued me.

With His own hands.

And whatever was to come next, I was no longer afraid.

The Farewell That Tore My Soul Apart.... Leaving Santo Domingo

The day of my departure arrived...

and the sky knew it.

The sun did not shine like on other afternoons.

It hid slowly behind heavy clouds that shed soft tears,

as if heaven itself resisted letting me go.

The air grew heavy.

And my soul was divided between the excitement of what was to come and the pain of everything I was leaving behind.

I was still in Santo Domingo.

My parents were in the town of Sánchez, Samaná.

And though my heart longed for one last embrace,

I could only hear them through the phone.

"I love you, daughter. May God keep you. You are going with a purpose."

My mother's voice was a whisper full of faith.

They were not many words, but they weighed like gold in my soul.

I hung up and sat in silence.

In my mind, I walked through the door of my home one last time.

I had not said goodbye physically, but at least I did so symbolically.

I knew that once I stepped outside that house, I would never be the same.

Then my sister Carmen Juana came to me.

She said nothing at first. She just looked at me.

And then she hugged me tightly.

A long hug.

Tight.

With the strength of someone who doesn't want to let go, but knows they must.

"Never forget who you are, Nuriss. You're not just a girl going there—you are being sent."

Her words engraved themselves into my skin.

Her eyes were full of love and of a serene faith,

that deep faith that only those who know God's power truly carry.

"Be strong. And when you feel alone, remember who sent you. God goes with you."

I couldn't respond.

I just cried.

But inside me... I made a promise:

I will not let her down.

That night was long.

I did not sleep.

There was a knot in my stomach that would not let me breathe.

I remembered every corner of my home.

Every voice.

Every prayer.

And at the same time, a different kind of excitement grew within me.

MY IMPACTFUL LIFE: FROM PAIN TO PURPOSE

God was sending me.

And I was going to obey.

The next morning, I left for Las Américas Airport.

My brother Julián, still just a young boy, came with me.

We got into a taxi that roared through the bustling streets of the city.

As we moved forward, every building, every traffic light, every street vendor spoke to me without words.

The warm wind of my land caressed my face.

And I let it... as if it were the island's last caress.

When we arrived at the airport, everything seemed too big.

Too new.

Too real.

The noise.

The voices.

The suitcases.

The announcements.

Everything was foreign.

Everything was intimidating.

But my faith… remained firm.

The farewell with Julián was the hardest.

He tried to stay strong, but his eyes betrayed him.

Mine too.

I didn't want him to see me weak, though the tears no longer asked for permission.

We hugged.

And in that embrace… I said goodbye to everything I knew.

"Take good care of yourself, Nuriss. I will be praying for you."

I nodded. Bowed my head.

Wiped my tears.

And walked in.

I went through immigration as if walking in a dream.

Everything seemed blurry.

MY IMPACTFUL LIFE: FROM PAIN TO PURPOSE

Everything felt heavy.

And when I reached the boarding area, I looked down and saw him.

My brother, standing on the second level, searching for me with his eyes.

I waved my hands to him.

And then, I broke.

I cried as if my soul were being torn in two.

Because I understood, in that moment, that I would not see them again for a long time.

And that now, I was completely in God's hands.

The plane had not yet taken off.

But I had already left the ground of my past.

And though my body was full of fear…

my spirit was already flying by faith.

Flight Into the Unknown

The airport unfolded before me like a monumental stage,

filled with strangers whose stories and destinies intertwined.

The smells of the terminal—a mixture of perfumes, food, and the tension of goodbyes—blended in the air.

Every corner was saturated with anticipation and nostalgia, creating an atmosphere both heavy and exhilarating.

My eyes blurred with sadness after saying goodbye to my brother Julián.

The pain of separation seized my heart,

and questions flooded my mind:

What will become of my life in Miami? Where will I sleep? Who will receive me?

My destiny was full of uncertainty,

and every step I took toward the plane deepened my anxiety.

I passed through immigration and walked to the passenger boarding area.

From there, I could see people on the upper level of the airport.

MY IMPACTFUL LIFE: FROM PAIN TO PURPOSE

I tried to spot my brother.

And when I finally found him in the distance,

tears of sorrow welled up in my eyes.

I waved goodbye with my hands.

I knew I would be far from my beloved family.

I boarded the plane and sat next to two women who noticed my pensive look.

The flight was announced as a journey into the unknown,

a passage that would take me through skies I had never even dreamed of.

The airplane lights flickered like shooting stars on the runway,

and my heart beat in rhythm with the engines roaring with power and determination.

As the plane lifted into the sky,

my gaze lingered on the lights fading in the distance.

The land I was leaving behind became a canvas of memories and experiences, but my mind was filled with expectations and longings for the future ahead.

The night skies bore witness to my journey,

and the stars aligned like celestial guides.

I sank into contemplation, reflecting on the road that had brought me here and the path that stretched before me.

Each star seemed to blink with a promise of hope,

reminding me that even though the way might be challenging,

I was being guided by something greater than myself.

The plane cut through the sky, breaking through thick clouds that seemed to whisper the secrets of the heavens.

From my window, I watched the world fall away behind me,

and with it, everything I knew.

My hands trembled.

It was my first time on a plane, and fear slid through my body like a cold current.

The hum of the engines thundered in my ears,

and every jolt tore out a held-back gasp.

My heart wasn't just beating...

it was pounding.

Thump. Thump. Thump.

As if it wanted to escape from my chest.

I looked around, seeking comfort in unfamiliar faces,

but no one seemed to notice I was on the verge of an inner collapse.

And just when I felt fear would consume me... something enveloped me.

An unexpected calm, profound,

like an invisible mantle descending over me, stilling the tremor of my soul.

It wasn't simple tranquility.

It was a peace that did not come from this world.

I closed my eyes, and for the first time in a long time...

I let go.

The destination no longer mattered.

Nor the fear.

Nor the uncertainty.

I only felt that I was in the air...

and in the right hands.

It was as if a force I couldn't see, but could feel,

took me by the hand and whispered in my ear:

"Be still. I am with you."

And I believed it. With all my being.

In that instant, I knew my life was being guided.

Not by coincidences, nor by human decisions...

but by a purpose greater than myself.

One only God knew.

One that was being fulfilled...

among the clouds.

Then, in the middle of the sky, as anxiety began to fade

and the vastness surrounded me, my heart beat with a new melody:

freedom and hope.

The hours in the air passed slowly, as if time stretched between the past left behind and the uncertain future awaiting me.

The soft cabin lights and the gentle hum of the engines wrapped me in a suspended atmosphere:

between heaven and earth, between the child I had been and the woman I did not yet know I would become.

The clouds stretched like a white mantle beneath the plane.

I gazed out the window in silence,

wondering if down there someone was thinking of me at that very moment.

I felt so alone...

but not abandoned.

I knew I was not traveling without company,

even if my emotions shook me inside.

I then remembered an address I often heard at home,

one repeated constantly on the Christian radio station *Radio Visión Cristiana*, based in Miami:

"P.O. Box."

That wasn't a house, nor a real place where anyone could receive me.

It was just a mailbox.

And with no other address, that was the one I wrote on the immigration form.

A simple mailbox.

The two women beside me, noticing my thoughtful state and young age, tried to speak with me.

When they realized I was traveling alone, one of them asked to see the address I had written down.

They looked at each other with concern.

"Child, this is a mailing address. It's not a place where someone can receive you," one of them told me gently.

I nodded timidly, trying to hide the fear beginning to course through me like a cold current.

I didn't want to admit it out loud, but I knew it:

there was no one waiting for me in Miami.

I had no contact.

MY IMPACTFUL LIFE: FROM PAIN TO PURPOSE

No plan.

Only faith.

And although in that moment the uncertainty was overwhelming,

an inner certainty remained firm, repeating the same phrase that had guided every one of my steps:

"Obey. I will show you what to do."

As the plane soared through the skies, I felt that each star outside shone like a promise.

One after another, they seemed to tell me not to give up.

That all of this had a greater purpose.

I closed my eyes, leaned against the window, and took a deep breath.

Because even though I did not know where I was going…

I knew with whom I was going.

I trusted.

I was literally being held by a force unseen…

A force that moved everything.

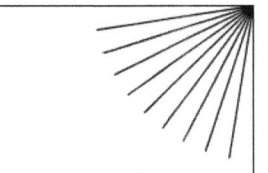

CHAPTER 5

Arrival in the United States – First Steps on Foreign Soil Miami and Arrival in New York: stations, trains, coldness, and disorientation

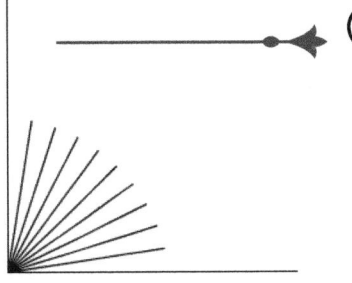

The sunset was timidly peeking over the horizon when the plane touched down in Miami.

The soft screech of the wheels on the runway pulled me out of the trance I had been in throughout the flight.

I opened my eyes slowly, as if my body already knew that by doing so, a new reality was about to begin.

The sky remained covered in bluish tones, but something inside me had changed.

I was no longer just a teenager traveling alone.

I was sent, fulfilling a calling.

But no matter how much purpose I carried, fear did not disappear.

The plane stopped, and the murmur of passengers filled the cabin.

Everyone seemed to know where they were going, whom they would see, what they would do upon arrival.

I didn't.

I stepped off the plane with my backpack in one hand

and uncertainty in the other.

The air felt different.

Not only because of the climate,

but because of the energy.

It was another world.

Everything around me was unfamiliar:

the faces, the languages, the sounds.

My eyes searched without finding.

There was no sign with my name.

No familiar face in the crowd.

No one waiting for me.

I walked toward baggage claim, pretending confidence.

But inside, my heart beat with desperation.

I pressed my lips together, swallowed hard, and remembered the address I had written on the immigration form:

a *P.O. Box* from Radio Visión Cristiana. A mailbox.

A place where only letters arrive. Not people.

The two women who had sat beside me on the flight came to me right away.

They looked at me with that mixture of tenderness and concern

that only kind souls know how to express.

"Where's your family? Who's here to meet you?"

I didn't know what to answer.

I lowered my gaze, and with a trembling voice, said:

"There's no one."

They looked at each other.

They didn't say much.

They didn't need to.

They acted with the urgency of someone who sees a sheep alone in an open field.

"We're not leaving you here alone, child. Tonight, you'll come with us. Tomorrow, we'll figure out what to do."

At that moment, something broke inside me—but not from fear.

It was relief.

The certainty that, once again,

God had sent help right on time.

They didn't know who I was.

But they knew Whom they served.

We left the airport and got into a car that seemed as foreign to me as everything else.

The streets of Miami paraded before my eyes with lights, signs, palm trees, and speed.

I said nothing. I only observed, swallowing my emotions.

That night, I slept in the home of two women heaven had placed in my path.

It wasn't my home.

They weren't my family.

But there was something in the atmosphere that made me feel safe.

Maybe I didn't have a plan…

But I had covering.

And that was more than enough.

The house was in Hialeah, Miami, and it belonged to the two Cuban women with whom I had shared the flight.

It was modest, quiet,

and though I was nervous,

I felt comfortable enough to rest there.

I didn't speak much.

My shyness kept me reserved,

as if my words had also traveled in silence.

I remember a small detail,

but one that was etched in my memory:

the refrigerator was white, and on it were colorful magnets, souvenirs, clipped papers, and little trinkets that seemed to tell family stories.

I sat on the sofa, my mind racing but my body demanding rest.

I slept. Not much, but I slept.

The next morning, around 10 a.m., they accompanied me back to the airport.

On the way, with a nervous smile, I told them perhaps my family would send me a return ticket to Santo Domingo.

That I would be fine... so they wouldn't worry further.

The hardest part was already behind me. I had been obedient.

And though I still didn't know how, my plan, together with the Lord, was to stay.

They left me in a waiting room.

They hugged me as if they had known me all their lives. And then they left.

And there I was... alone again.

I began walking back and forth.

Aimless. Clueless.

As if each step were an unanswered question.

The airport was a universe of its own:

people in a hurry, children crying, announcements echoing, luggage, unfamiliar languages.

I got lost among them, trying to go unnoticed.

I remembered the words of Psalm 23:

"The Lord is my shepherd, I shall not want."

And with that promise echoing in my soul, I prayed.

I prayed like someone who has no other option.

I prayed with faith… but also with fear.

Because even though I trusted that God would not leave me alone,

I feared that at any moment someone would notice.

That the airport authorities would realize I had no one, that I was underage,

and send me back to my country.

My heart raced.

My hands sweated.

And my eyes scanned everything,

trying to appear secure.

But inside,

I felt suspended in time.

I didn't know how to get to New York.

I had no plan.

I only had that burning faith...

because at that moment,

it was the only thing I had in a world that seemed to move without me.

And yet...

in the middle of all that chaos, in the midst of noise, departures, and arrivals...

I was still there. Standing.

Because though I was alone... I was not abandoned.

God was still writing my story.

And this was only the next chapter.

At the Miami Airport with $32 and a Dream

Night had already taken over the Miami airport.

The cold lights shone on the polished floors,

and the crowd moved like a human river that never stopped.

I, on the other hand, was stranded.

Suspended between the past I had left behind in Santo Domingo

and the uncertain future that had yet to be revealed.

With only $32 in my pocket—the very same my mother had given me with so much sacrifice—

I had already spent a few dollars on a simple orange juice.

The cold of the juice contrasted with the sadness burning inside me.

I sat in a corner, hugging my backpack—my only refuge—

and brought the paper cup to my lips as I watched people passing by.

Every person seemed to have a destination, a home, a story to follow.

I only had the echo of God's promise resonating in my heart.

But the fear was real.

Uncertainty tightened my chest,

and tears began to fall silently, one by one,

like confessions no one would hear.

As I sipped that juice—the most expensive and painful one I had ever tasted—

I looked at the crowd with a mixture of hope and despair.

If only someone would come near me… if only someone would say, "Come to my house, I'll give you a corner to sleep in and something to eat," I thought, heartbroken.

I was nervous. Very nervous.

A teenage girl, alone, foreign, without family, without an address, without money.

A new country.

A different language.

A city as immense as a shoreless ocean.

MY IMPACTFUL LIFE: FROM PAIN TO PURPOSE

I felt small.

Invisible.

But still... determined to endure.

I knew I couldn't stay there forever.

That the money wouldn't last even for the next day's breakfast.

That sleeping on a bench wasn't an option.

But what else could I do?

I cried.

I cried like a girl missing her mother, her father, her sisters.

I cried for the courage that pushed me to board that plane without knowing exactly where I would end up.

I cried because I didn't know if I would survive.

But even crying, even trembling...

I knew I couldn't give up.

Because inside me,

a soft yet powerful voice kept whispering:

Endure. I am with you.

And so, with an empty stomach, a trembling soul, and a heart burning with faith,

I wiped my tears, picked up my backpack, and prepared to keep going.

I didn't know how or when,

but I knew one thing:

God hadn't brought me this far to abandon me.

Night had fallen over the Miami airport,

and with it, the weight of exhaustion pressed on my shoulders.

The fluorescent ceiling lights buzzed monotonously,

and the air conditioning kept blowing indifferently,

as if it didn't care that I—a teenage girl,

directionless, was sitting there trying to survive the exhaustion, the cold, and the uncertainty.

My feet ached.

My body was exhausted.

MY IMPACTFUL LIFE: FROM PAIN TO PURPOSE

My eyelids fell like worn-out shutters.

I was completely drained.

I curled up on one of the long benches, hugging my backpack, which at that moment was all I had.

I closed my eyes and let myself be carried away by exhaustion,

by the desire to disappear, at least for a few hours, from the pain that pressed against my chest.

On that bench, surrounded by strangers coming and going,

I fell asleep.

I don't know how much time passed,

but suddenly, a soft yet firm voice woke me,

like a ray of reality piercing my sleep:

"Are you alright?"

I opened my eyes, disoriented.

In front of me stood a woman in uniform, an airport employee.

Her eyes looked at me with a mix of concern and authority.

"Yes…" I answered weakly, trying to show strength.

"Don't you have anywhere to go?"

I shook my head gently, swallowing the lump in my throat.

"No… I don't have anywhere to go."

She bent slightly, lowering herself to my level.

"You can't stay here, sweetheart. You need to call someone to come get you."

I wanted to reply,

but I had no one to call.

I had no family in that state.

No address.

No clear destination.

I was alone. Completely alone.

At that moment, I felt as though the ground opened beneath my feet.

But even in the midst of anguish,

something inside reminded me I was not alone:

God was still with me.

While she waited for my response, I could only pray silently:

"Lord, what do I do now?

Show me the way…"

Whom could I call?

I had no phone.

No address.

I didn't know anyone in Miami.

All I had were my dreams

and the word God had given me days before.

But in that moment,

even the strongest promise seemed to fade against the cold floor of reality.

I tried to remain composed, but inside I felt small, broken.

A minor, alone in another country,

without resources, without a destination.

The only thing I had was my faith.

I looked at the woman and lowered my eyes.

She didn't insist further.

She just stood there a few seconds, as if waiting for something to happen.

And something did.

Inside me, a gentle voice, almost imperceptible, spoke clearly:

"Do not be afraid. I am with you."

The same voice that had spoken to me that night in Santo Domingo.

I felt warmth in my chest.

As if an invisible blanket covered me for a few seconds.

I had no plan,

but I had God.

And that gave me strength.

I stayed there for a few minutes, thinking what to do,

waiting for a sign, an idea, a person.

And it was there,

in the middle of my desperation,

that the story took another turn.

A Door Opens to my destiny

After that encounter with the airport woman and the bittersweet sip of that orange juice,

my thoughts raced as quickly as the planes that kept taking off.

I felt so small in the middle of the crowd,

like a leaf in the middle of a storm.

Tears slid down silently as I told myself:

I can't give up now... I came from so far. This cannot be the end.

The airport's public phone hung from a worn-out wall.

Next to it, I held my last coins as if they were gold.

I had spent the whole night awake, with no place to go,

my eyes swollen from so much crying.

The echo of flight announcements filled the air,

but none of them were for me.

Once more, I approached the public phone.

My hands trembled as I lifted the receiver.

With my heart squeezed tight, I dialed a collect call to Santo Domingo—

to my sister Carmen Juana.

When I heard her voice, my soul broke.

I couldn't hold back the tears.

"Carmen Juana… I don't know what to do. I'm at the airport… and I have nowhere to go," I said, swallowing my sobs.

There was a silence that weighed like tons.

"Listen to me, Nuriss," she finally said with determination.

"I remember that Luisa, our Uncle Antonio's wife, gave us the number of her sister who lives in New York. Her name is Dolores… I don't know what she's like, but call her. Call her right now! Maybe she can help you."

Dolores? Call a stranger, a name without a face?

How could I ask for help from someone who didn't even know me?

But I had no other choice.

Only faith. Faith that God would move her heart.

With the little change I had left, I dialed the number my sister gave me.

I called collect. The phone rang once, twice... but no one answered.

My soul hovered at the edge of despair.

The exhaustion, the hunger, the uncertainty... were crushing me inside.

I tried again.

And again.

And again.

I felt desperate,

like a boat about to sink.

Until finally... someone picked up the receiver.

"Hello?"

"Is this Dolores?" I asked with a trembling voice.

"This is Nuriss, niece of Antonio, your sister Luisa's husband. I'm at the Miami airport… I have nowhere to go… They told me maybe you could help me get to New York."

There was a long silence.

"You're there alone?" she asked, doubting.

"Yes. I have no family here. I just… I just want to get to New York. I promise, if you help me, I will work, I'll do whatever it takes. I just need a safe place and a chance."

The pause felt eternal.

My heart seemed to stop.

Then, her voice changed.

It became warmer. More human.

"Give me a few minutes. Call me later."

Hours later, after more calls and silent prayers,

she finally said:

"I'm going to call the airline. If I can arrange to send you the ticket, I'll have it delivered to the counter. Be alert."

"Really? You would do that for me?" I asked, choking on a lump in my throat.

"Yes, child. I'll help you. Tell me what you're wearing so I can recognize you when you arrive."

"I'm wearing a green-blue skirt with little pink flowers."

The miracle happened.

Dolores agreed to help me.

My legs trembled.

My heart pounded wildly.

I couldn't believe it.

I hung up. I stood in front of the phone, lifted my head, and whispered:

"Thank You, Lord... I know You are working."

Hours dragged on after that call.

Every minute felt like a year.

I sat near the waiting area, hugging my blue backpack as if it were my only friend.

I was exhausted.

But not defeated.

My gaze fixed on the airport's automatic doors,

where hundreds of people walked out with destination, with family, with plans…

everything I didn't have.

Finally, I felt a prompting in my spirit.

I stood up and walked to the airline counter.

"Excuse me… is there a ticket reserved under the name Nuriss?"

The agent typed slowly.

I could barely breathe.

Then she looked up and said:

"Yes. Here it is. Your ticket to New York is confirmed. It was just paid for by a lady named Dolores."

It was real!

I jumped with joy, unable to contain myself.

I clutched the ticket to my chest and cried.

I cried with joy.

I cried with relief.

The ticket in my hands wasn't just a piece of paper:

it was living proof that heaven had moved in my favor.

Overwhelmed with emotion, I stepped aside, held the ticket like a treasure,

and, looking toward heaven, whispered:

"Thank You, Lord... You have not left me."

I finally called my sister Carmen Juana:

"I'm going! I have the ticket! Dolores sent it to me."

Her joyful cry on the other end of the line was my confirmation.

"Glory to the Lord! She's going North! Nuriss is going to New York!"

As I hung up, I looked up at the sky through the airport windows:

"Here begins the true journey, Lord, with You."

When my name was called over the loudspeakers,

I stood up, my hands still sweating,

and walked to the boarding gate with the ticket clutched tightly between my fingers,

like a sacred treasure.

The plane began to rise.

The runway grew small.

The lights of Miami faded away.

This wasn't the end.

It was only the beginning.

I cried silently.

As I gazed at the golden sky,

I knew that the teenage girl who had slept on cold benches,

who had had no ticket,

was now flying, sustained by God's invisible hand.

The city of New York awaited me…

and with it, a new chapter of faith, struggle, and purpose.

Arrival in New York

I felt my heart rise to my throat.

Three hours later, the plane landed in a city I only knew through photos and movies.

New York.

I wore the same skirt I had described to Dolores on the phone:

a green-blue skirt with little pink flowers.

It was my only signal of identity...

my only way of being recognized upon landing.

I carried no suitcases.

Only a blue backpack on my shoulders,

small but loaded with dreams, faith, and resilience.

The plane taxied along the runway at John F. Kennedy International Airport.

Through the window, all I could see were lights, fog, and massive metallic structures.

Everything seemed to move at a different rhythm.

as if the world here ran faster than anywhere else on the planet.

When I stepped off the plane,

the human tide engulfed me.

Men, women, children, rolling suitcases, voices in English over the loudspeakers…

Everything was confusing. Overwhelming.

People walked with purpose, knowing exactly where they were going.

I, on the other hand, didn't even know who to look for.

I let myself be carried along by the crowd,

following the steps of others,

hoping that instinct—and God—would guide me.

When we reached baggage claim, everyone began to scatter.

Some stopped at the conveyor belts, others embraced family members.

And I… I was left alone.

I remembered that Dolores would be there, along with her

husband Andrés, holding a sign with her name.

But I didn't know what she looked like, nor her husband.

The only thing they knew about me was that I was wearing a green-blue skirt with little pink flowers.

I stood by a column, trying not to be in the way, while people rushed around me.

Nerves took hold of me.

What if they don't find me?

What if they came and didn't see me?

Each time someone lifted a sign, I stretched to see if it said "Dolores" or "Nuriss."

But nothing. The minutes felt like hours.

I started walking in circles, scanning faces, clothing, glances—

not even sure what I was searching for.

The air felt heavy, and my throat was dry.

Then suddenly, I saw a couple standing near the exit.

The man, older, with a kind face;

the woman, younger, holding a small sign that simply said:

"Dolores."

I approached slowly, almost trembling.

She looked me up and down. Her face lit up.

"Are you Nuriss?" she asked, with a smile that brought my soul back to life.

"Yes... I'm her," I replied in a faint voice.

Then she came close and hugged me warmly.

Relief flooded me like a torrent.

Andrés welcomed me with a shy smile and took my blue backpack.

Dolores looked at me as if she had known me all her life.

"I knew it was you because of the skirt," she said, laughing softly.

"That was our clue!"

And so, between hugs and shy smiles, we left the airport together.

The automatic doors slid open in front of me,

and New York's cold air greeted me with its first breath.

MY IMPACTFUL LIFE: FROM PAIN TO PURPOSE

The Bronx seemed noisy, gray, and unfamiliar.

The buildings were tall, the streets endless, the elevated trains roared above my head.

At every corner, hurried people, faces from many cultures.

And I, with my flowered skirt and blue backpack,

felt like a drop in an immense ocean.

In the car, Dolores and Andrés chatted,

but my eyes couldn't leave the window.

I saw bright storefronts, street vendors, yellow taxis multiplying by the dozen.

I had never seen a city so alive.

When we arrived at the building where they lived, we climbed creaking stairs.

The modest second-floor apartment became my first refuge in this unfamiliar land.

They showed me the living room where I would sleep. It wasn't much, but to me, it was a palace.

They welcomed me kindly, though their eyes reflected a hint of suspicion.

They didn't know me. I didn't know how long I could stay.

But that night, I had a roof. And that was enough.

Through the window, the city lights flickered, stirring my thoughts.

New York vibrated, moved, spoke to me...

and even though I felt so small, I knew I was part of something bigger.

My blue backpack carried more dreams than clothes.

Inside me lived the unshakable conviction that God had a plan.

I sat on the couch.

The accumulated exhaustion of endless days weighed on my shoulders.

As I listened to the rumble of the train and the unending sirens,

I thought of Santo Domingo.

Of my mother.

Of my sisters.

Of the wooden church.

Of my street, Calle Sánchez.

And I understood:

this place was a concrete jungle...

but if God had brought me here,

it was because He had a purpose.

I hugged myself, closed my eyes, and whispered:

"Lord, I don't understand all of this, but I trust You."

My body couldn't go on any longer.

I leaned back on the couch.

And before I knew it...

I fell into a deep sleep,

the kind that only comes when the soul has been hanging by a thread all day.

And that's how,

in the middle of a city that never sleeps,

a young immigrant girl began to write her new story.

Stranger in the Big City

I woke up on the couch in Dolores's apartment in the Bronx,

with the gray light of dawn filtering through the window.

For a moment, I didn't know where I was.

My body still remembered the cold of the airport,

the weight of the blue backpack on my shoulders,

the trembling of uncertainty.

But here I was. In a new home. In a city I didn't know. New York.

I slowly sat up.

The apartment was quiet.

Dolores and her husband were already awake, busy with their routines.

They greeted me kindly,

but the air was filled with that tension that comes with the unexpected.

It wasn't easy for them to have a teenage stranger in their

home.

And it wasn't easy for me...

to be a stranger in that place.

That day began like a blank page.

From the window, I watched the cars going back and forth,

the voices speaking in English, the frantic movement of the city.

Everything was so fast. So foreign.

I, who came from a small town where you could hear the birds in the morning

and church songs at night,

was now surrounded by gray buildings, constant noise,

and sidewalks filled with people who didn't see me.

I felt small.

Invisible.

But not broken.

Even though my eyes filled silently with tears,

even though my throat ached from holding them back,

even though I missed my family and my country with every fiber of my being…

I knew I wasn't alone. The Lord was with me.

And in my heart, the echo of His promise kept repeating:

"I will be with you wherever you go."

During those first days, I tried not to bother Dolores.

I stayed in the living room, quiet, orderly.

I offered to help, though many times she said it wasn't necessary.

My mind couldn't stop asking:

What now?

What comes next?

Where will I go?

How long will they let me stay here?

But something inside me reminded me:

this was only one more step.

Every night on that couch,

every glance out the window,

every whispered prayer...

was part of a process I had to go through.

That's how my life in New York began.

Without school.

Without family.

Without certainties.

But with something stronger than all of that:

a hope planted in new soil.

First Impressions of the Iron Giant

New York...

the very giant of concrete, steel, and dreams.

From the moment I left the airport and came face to face with the city,

I knew I was in a completely different world.

Everything moved so fast. The cars. The trains. The people.

Everyone seemed to run under the pressure of time.

The skyscrapers rose imposingly toward the sky,

like giant hands defying the clouds.

I looked up and it seemed they never ended.

The air was cold,

carrying the smell of street food, smoke, and something metallic.

I felt a mix of excitement and fear…

as if my heart shouted,

"At last, you made it!"

and at the same time whispered,

"Get ready, because this won't be easy."

The signs in English overwhelmed me.

I understood almost nothing, but I tried to decipher what I could.

The lights.

MY IMPACTFUL LIFE: FROM PAIN TO PURPOSE

The car horns.

The constant murmur of the subway underground...

It was a chaotic symphony that, little by little, I began to accept

as the new soundtrack of my life.

I remember that while we drove toward the Bronx, where I would stay at first,

I stared out the window wide-eyed,

as if I wanted to absorb every detail.

Snow piled up on the corners,

and the trees were bare from winter.

I felt tiny among so many buildings.

But at the same time... alive.

More alive than ever.

I didn't understand much,

but I understood this: I had arrived.

I had arrived in the city where anything is possible.

The city that welcomed me and challenged me at the same time.

The days in the Bronx began to pass slowly, cold, and silent.

My routine was simple: wake up early, help where I could, look out the window, pray quietly.

Sometimes I spent the whole day in the living room,

with my blue backpack at my side,

as if it were my only anchor.

Dolores and her husband were kind, but also reserved.

They didn't ask me questions,

and I didn't say much either.

I felt like an accidental visitor,

a guest of destiny.

The voices in the neighborhood were different.

The music, the language, the way people walked.

Everything was new.

Sometimes I peeked out the window just to watch life go by.

MY IMPACTFUL LIFE: FROM PAIN TO PURPOSE

Children ran along the sidewalks,

mothers pushed strollers,

elders sat on the stoops of buildings.

And I... stood behind the glass.

The nights were the hardest.

Nostalgia captured me without asking permission.

I thought of my mother, my sister Carmen Juana, my brother Julián,

my sisters Rosa Chovy and María Belkis.

And I wondered if they were alright.

Sometimes I cried silently when everyone was asleep.

Not from weakness.

But because my soul needed space to let go.

But in the midst of those gray days...

there was something that never went out:

my faith.

Every morning, before the sun came up,

I knelt by the couch.

With the Bible in my hands and my heart trembling,

I spoke to the Lord.

I told Him my fears. My doubts. My longings.

And though I had no clear answers,

I felt His presence like a current wrapping around me.

"You are not alone. This too shall pass."

One day, while I was helping to clean the kitchen a bit,

Dolores looked at me.

She asked softly:

"Do you have a plan? Do you know where you want to go?"

I stayed silent for a few seconds.

Then I replied:

"I don't know yet. I only know that God does."

I didn't have a map.

I didn't have human promises.

But I had spiritual direction.

And in that time of uncertainty,

God was preparing the ground.

I didn't know it then...

but the next turn was closer than I imagined.

Something Begins to Move...
My True Journey in New York

The days kept passing in that Bronx apartment,

marked by the sound of traffic,

the echo of footsteps on the stairwell,

and the unchanging routine of those who worked hard just to survive.

I watched from the living room,

surrounded by books, prayers, and thoughts that sometimes weighed heavier than the city itself.

Something deep within me began to stir.

It wasn't a voice.

It wasn't a revealing dream.

It was more like a sacred unease.

As if God was gently nudging me from the inside.

As if He was whispering:

"I didn't bring you here to sit still."

One afternoon, while clearing some dishes in the kitchen,

I overheard a conversation between Dolores and her husband.

They spoke in low voices,

but I caught a phrase:

"She needs something to do... something that will give her strength back."

That phrase echoed in my mind.

It hurt a little, but it also woke me up.

Was I fading?

Was I starting to forget who I was

and all that I had already overcome?

That night, in prayer, I told the Lord:

MY IMPACTFUL LIFE: FROM PAIN TO PURPOSE

"If it's time for me to move... show me.

If there's something for me, open a door.

I don't want to remain still.

I am ready."

I prayed with an open heart, without conditions.

Just eager to surrender.

And the very next day... something happened.

Dolores asked me if I wanted to go out with her,

to run some errands around the city.

It wasn't much... Yet for me, it meant everything.

I changed clothes as if I were getting ready for an important appointment.

I combed my hair more carefully than usual.

I looked at my reflection in the mirror and, for the first time since I had arrived,

I saw a spark in my eyes.

I stepped out into the street and felt the air on my face like a new breath.

NURISS CLARK

The sounds were the same,

but now I heard them differently.

I was no longer just a lost teenager.

I was a daughter of God in motion.

We went to several places.

She showed me how basic things worked,

how to read the street names,

how to move around the neighborhood.

It was as if I were being born again…

but in a completely unfamiliar land.

As we walked through the streets of the Bronx,

I felt that each step marked a new beginning.

Each corner was a possibility.

Each crossing, a decision.

And though I didn't yet know where it would all lead…

I felt that something had begun.

MY IMPACTFUL LIFE: FROM PAIN TO PURPOSE

It wasn't a giant change, nor a thunderous miracle.

It was the beginning of something that would no longer stop.

God had begun to move pieces…

and I was willing to follow His rhythm.

The silence was beginning to break.

And my soul was beginning to walk.

A few days later, Dolores—the woman who had taken me in without truly knowing me—

spoke to me firmly:

"Go ahead, you can go downstairs and walk around the neighborhood."

Before I left, she handed me an old coat she had kept in storage.

It was a bit too big,

the sleeves nearly covering my hands,

but in that New York cold, it was a blessing.

I didn't care that it didn't fit perfectly;

what mattered was that it kept me warm… and in that moment, that was everything I needed.

I went out to walk through the neighborhood.

I saw the streets, the names at the corners,

and nearby stood the East Tremont Avenue station,

where the 2, 5, B, and D trains passed.

I walked up to the subway entrance, stared at it in wonder, and whispered to myself:

"That's where you go in. Dolores already told you, you have to buy a token—a kind of coin used instead of a ticket—that lets you pass through the turnstiles and ride the train. It's simple."

But I didn't enter the subway station.

I just stood there at the staircase,

caught between nerves, fear, and an unusual determination beginning to rise within me.

I didn't know how to read the map,

or how to figure out which stop was correct,

or how to identify the trains.

I only knew one thing: I had to learn.

No one else could do it for me.

That was the first and only time Dolores gave me any kind of guidance on how things worked in New York.

From that day on, the learning was mine.

And so began my true journey in New York.

One that was not only physical, but also spiritual.

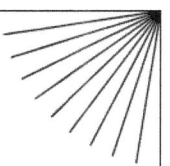

CHAPTER 6

**When Everything Became Clouded
Loneliness, factory, heartbreaking
letter, snow, sleeping on the train,
night of despair, asking for 5 cents to
eat, at the edge of death**

My First Time Out Alone in New York

I stayed a little longer at Dolores' house.

She tried to help me, though it was clear it wasn't easy.

She did what she could to find me some kind of work,

a door that might open...

But I was just a small teenager.

And in the United States, teenagers could only work a few hours in the summer or after school. Doors didn't open for them.

They closed quietly,

like a light being switched off without sound.

Dolores looked at me with compassion.

I was small, thin, shy... barely a whisper.

I seemed more fragile than I really was.

And maybe that's why no one took me seriously.

"You're too young, too little... here they don't give jobs to girls like you," she once said, trying not to hurt me, though reality has no disguise.

But she insisted.

She spoke to some acquaintances who had a factory.

It had only been a few days since I'd ventured out to the neighborhood and seen the train station.

One morning, as I ate breakfast in silence, she said:

"I spoke with some friends. They'll give you a job in a factory. It's sewing clothes, nothing too complicated. You start tomorrow."

I nodded with a timid smile, though inside I didn't know how to react.

I didn't understand how factories worked,

nor what kind of effort sewing required.

But I knew one thing:

I needed to do something. And I couldn't say no.

That night I couldn't sleep well.

My stomach ached from nerves.

The next morning, very early, Dolores explained how to get there.

She didn't go with me.

She handed me a slip of paper with the address and gave me a few coins for the bus.

"You get on here, and get off there. Ask if you get lost," she said quickly.

I took the bus alone for the first time.

I sat by the window, clutching the paper with the address between my fingers.

Everything was new. The streets, the signs in English, the announcements over the loudspeaker.

My legs trembled.

I felt like a child wandering in an unknown world.

When I arrived, the factory was a gray building, with no visible windows.

The air smelled of fabric, steam, and sweat.

They gave me a uniform, an old machine,

and pointed silently to where I should sit.

The job was to sew the same piece over and over again.

Over and over. The same fabric. The same seam.

The same relentless noise of the machines.

The atmosphere was hostile.

The women spoke English and other languages I didn't recognize.

I kept to myself. Observed. Tried to follow the pace.

But the needles, the threads, the speed… it was too much for me.

My hands shook. I pricked my fingers several times.

My neck felt stiff, my eyes clouded.

By midday, I could barely swallow the small lunch I had brought.

I felt small. Out of place. Incapable.

I lasted two days.

Just two days my body and soul endured.

I went with hope.

MY IMPACTFUL LIFE: FROM PAIN TO PURPOSE

With illusion.

With faith.

But as soon as I walked through the door,

the environment overwhelmed me.

The noise of the machines was deafening.

The smell of metal, the sweat, the shouting, the speed…

everything felt unreal, like a nightmare I couldn't wake from.

My body couldn't resist.

My hands trembled.

My muscles tensed.

My eyes blurred more with each passing hour.

I endured one day.

I returned the second.

And that's when I realized I couldn't go on.

I leaned against a wall.

A tear rolled down my cheek.

Not from weakness. From helplessness.

I wanted to help. I wanted to stand on my own.

But that job wasn't for me.

I walked out of the factory with my head lowered,

my arms aching,

and my soul staggering.

I returned home with tearful eyes.

I told Dolores I couldn't continue.

That I had tried, but I couldn't go on.

She looked at me, pressed her lips together, and didn't say much.

Maybe she thought I was weak.

Perhaps she was right.

But deep inside, I knew that wasn't my battle.

That wasn't my place.

I felt ashamed. I felt useless.

But I also understood that not everything is achieved by force.

Sometimes, it isn't about giving up,

but about recognizing that some paths don't belong to us.

That was my first job in New York.

My first attempt.

And also, my first failure.

Yet I knew that God had something greater for me.

That night... I didn't eat dinner.

I wasn't hungry.

But more than that,

I had no will.

I locked myself in the small bathroom of the apartment,

the only place where I could be alone, if only for a few minutes.

I shut the door, sat on the toilet lid, and hugged my knees.

I cried in silence. Softly.

I didn't want anyone to hear me.

I didn't want to bother.

I didn't want to be a burden.

But something inside me broke.

I covered my face with my hands and began to pray,

to speak with the only One who truly knew how I felt.

"Lord, is this why You brought me here?

For this? To fail, to be useless, to hurt, to struggle...?"

The loneliness grew heavier as the tears fell.

The voice of my thoughts told me maybe I had made a mistake.

And in the middle of those doubts, in that silent bathroom... something happened.

It wasn't a voice.

It wasn't a word.

It was a sensation... soft... like a whisper from within.

As if someone were hugging me from the inside.

MY IMPACTFUL LIFE: FROM PAIN TO PURPOSE

It wasn't explainable.

It wasn't visible.

But it was real.

A strength that didn't come from me held me up inside.

As if heaven itself whispered:

"This is not it. But keep going. Don't stop."

My tears kept falling,

but my heart, though broken, began to heal.

I wiped my face with the back of my hand,

took a deep breath,

and knew I had to keep moving.

That wasn't my end.

It was just another step on the journey.

I walked out of the bathroom without saying a word.

No one asked.

No one noticed.

But I knew something had shifted.

Something inside me had been rekindled.

Silence in the Apartment

Nearly three weeks went by.

I was still there, in that borrowed apartment,

helping in whatever way I could to earn my keep.

Dolores wasn't very talkative,

but she allowed me to stay as long as I cleaned, picked up, swept, or sometimes cooked.

I didn't want to be a burden.

I only wanted her to let me stay, while I figured out my path.

Each day looked just like the one before.

Meals arrived sometimes with few words—

a plate on the table, a brief gesture.

Other times, absolute silence.

I ate slowly,

like someone grateful for every bite,

like someone who understood she was living on mercy.

The nights were the longest.

The television murmured softly in the living room.

Outside, the Bronx stayed alive with distant sirens,

speeding cars,

and that constant hum of a city that never sleeps.

Sometimes I woke up early

just to look out the window and see how the city began to stir awake.

I felt like a shadow inside that place.

Invisible.

Suspended between who I had been… and who I didn't yet know I was becoming.

There were no reproaches.

No deep conversations. Only small gestures.

But the silences—those weighed more than any word.

I felt the invisible weight of being there.

I felt the days piling up like dry leaves no one came to gather.

My prayer was constant:

Lord, don't let me get stuck here.

Move me when the time is right.

And it was in those days of routine,

in the echo of silence and the whisper of my nightly prayers,

that I began to feel something different:

a restlessness. A whisper in the soul.

As if God were already preparing the stage…

for the next chapter.

I didn't know what was coming.

I only knew I had to remain firm—

in prayer, in service, and with a willing heart.

Because even though the apartment was silent…

in heaven, the pieces were already moving.

The Letter That Broke My Heart and Shattered My Soul

Several days went by.

I kept doing everything I could to earn my keep at Dolores's apartment.

I helped her clean, tidied up the kitchen, swept the hallways, folded laundry.

She didn't ask me to, but I did it… because I knew I was living off her generosity.

One ordinary afternoon, while straightening her room,

I saw a letter near the mirror, right where I always dusted.

That letter wasn't for me.

It didn't have my name on it.

It hadn't been placed in my hands.

But there it was… open.

As if it had been waiting for me.

I stepped closer slowly,

as if I already knew that what I was about to read would change something inside me.

I immediately recognized the name on the envelope.

It was from Santo Domingo.

From my own uncle: Antonio.

The same one whose wife, Luisa, had given me the contact number.

The same one who knew I was alone in the United States.

My eyes began to follow the lines written on the page.

At first, I didn't fully understand.

But as I kept reading,

the words grew harsher, colder, sharper.

"I heard that Nuriss is staying at your house…"

My hands started to tremble.

"…But we don't agree with that."

"That family is too problematic."

"You don't have to let her live with you."

I froze.

The paper shook in my fingers.

My heart pounded so hard it was difficult to breathe.

What had I done wrong?

Why was he rejecting me like this?

The ground seemed to open beneath my feet.

The air grew heavy.

Tears started to fall, one after another, hot, heavy, unstoppable.

My own uncle... was rejecting me.

Calling me a burden. A problem. An intruder.

I pressed the letter to my chest and slowly sat on the edge of the sofa,

clutching it while the tears kept streaming.

I didn't understand.

I couldn't comprehend how someone of my own blood could speak of me that way—

without knowing my pain,

without knowing the nights of cold, of hunger, of loneliness, of fear...

In that moment, I understood why Dolores had grown distant,

why her words had become scarce,

why her eyes avoided mine.

She hadn't said it aloud.

She didn't have the courage.

But she left the letter open,

as if speaking through a cowardly silence.

I felt invisible.

Alone.

Broken.

It wasn't just the distance.

It was rejection from those who shared my blood.

And that kind of rejection hurts in a different way... a deeper way.

MY IMPACTFUL LIFE: FROM PAIN TO PURPOSE

That night I couldn't sleep.

Every time I closed my eyes,

the words from that letter repeated in my mind like a cruel hammer.

But in the midst of the pain and the tears, I knelt down.

"Lord... if even family turns their back on me,

then let it be You who opens the doors.

I don't want to depend on anyone else.

I only want to depend on You."

And while the Bronx slept,

a frail teenage girl with a blue backpack and a shattered soul

laid her pain before the only One who would never reject her.

I looked at myself in the mirror, the same mirror where I had found the letter,

and I didn't recognize the girl staring back at me.

But just when I thought I couldn't take it anymore...

I remembered what God had told me:

I will show you what you must do.

It wasn't the end.

It was another test.

I wiped my tears.

Folded the letter carefully, as if closing a wound,

placed it back where I had found it.

And I stood up.

Hurt, yes.

But stronger than ever.

Because even when men close the doors on you...

when God decides to bless you, no letter, no word, no man can stop it.

Beneath the Snow, Aimless and with a Burning Soul

After reading that letter... something inside me broke.

It wasn't just pain.

It was a silent tearing, a mixture of anguish, anger, disappointment, and loneliness so intense that I could hardly breathe.

I cried.

Not a single tear, not a quiet sob.

I cried like a child abandoned in the middle of the world.

And the worst part was... it was true.

I was alone.

Without a place of my own, without an embrace, without a guaranteed plate of food.

I couldn't bear to look at Dolores, or her husband, or even at the mirror.

I needed to run.

To let that knot in my chest spill out, even if it was just by walking… aimlessly.

I put on the first thing I found, grabbed my blue backpack… and left.

It was winter.

It was snowing.

Not a gentle, postcard snowfall.

It was one of those storms that fall as if the sky itself were crying with me.

The snow struck my face, seeped into my shoes, covered my legs,

soaked my ankles, froze my thoughts.

But I didn't stop.

I walked.

And walked.

And walked.

I had no map.

No plan.

No destination.

Just a broken heart and two feet that refused to stay where they were not welcome.

My hands froze inside the pockets of a borrowed coat.

Each step sank into the snow up to my calves.

But the cold outside was nothing compared to the cold I felt in my soul.

My thoughts screamed:

—Why, Lord?

—What did I do wrong?

—Why do they abandon me?

—Why am I always the one who has to endure?

But there was no answer.

Only snow.

Only cold.

Only the Bronx.

I stopped at a corner.

Looked around and recognized nothing.

I was completely lost.

But inside... a spark—

a barely visible spark—began to ignite.

Because in the middle of the snow, the abandonment, and the sorrow...

I knew I was still alive.

And if I was alive... there was still purpose.

An inner force, one that wasn't mine, pushed me:

Keep going. Don't stop. This too shall pass.

I kept walking until I reached the East Tremont Avenue train station.

I stood at the corner, frozen, watching from a distance as if time itself had stopped.

It was the first time I ever boarded the subway in New York.

Everything was noisy, fast, unknown.

I felt small, fragile, invisible.

MY IMPACTFUL LIFE: FROM PAIN TO PURPOSE

I watched how people lined up to buy small metal tokens.

They placed them in the turnstile and walked to the other side.

I didn't know how it worked… but I learned by watching.

I took a deep breath.

Stepped forward.

Pulled a few trembling coins from my pocket and bought my very first token.

It was round, with a tiny hole in the center.

But to me… it was more than just a fare.

It was my first step toward independence.

I slid the token into the turnstile.

Pushed.

Crossed.

On the other side there wasn't just a train…

There was my new life.

That day, without anyone teaching me, I learned how to take the train in New York.

And I also learned that, even in the midst of snow, confusion, and pain...

one can always take the first step.

Because even when I felt lost...

God was still guiding my steps.

The Night on the Train... in the Shadows of the Subway

Anguish and despair took hold of me.

It was as if the cold didn't just freeze my skin...

but also my soul.

It was 6:00 p.m.

I was at the train station.

The noise of metal surrounded me:

pra-pra-pra-pra.

I waited... but not because I was in a hurry.

I had nowhere to go.

MY IMPACTFUL LIFE: FROM PAIN TO PURPOSE

No home waiting for me.

No roof.

No family.

I carried my subway map, that small folded piece of paper that had become my only guide, my only plan.

I stared at it... without really knowing what I was looking for.

I looked at people.

At the ground.

At the sky.

—Oh Father... alone and forsaken.

I walked to the far end of the station, where there were fewer people.

Everything was darker.

Quieter.

Sadder.

I sat on one of the benches, lowered my head... and faced the truth:

Tonight, I had no roof.

I knew it.

I felt it.

I feared it.

I would have to take refuge in the train cars.

Those cold, dirty, unsafe places…

where smells, dangers, and lost souls mix together.

That's where I would sleep.

A teenage girl, with a blue backpack and a few belongings.

Me… alone in New York.

My heart wanted to leap out of my chest.

It pounded so hard it hurt to breathe.

"Do I really have to sleep in there?" I whispered, crying softly, trying not to make noise among strangers.

What happens in those subway cars… I wouldn't wish on anyone.

There are addicts, people with empty eyes, men who look at you as if you weren't even human.

The floor is filthy, sticky.

MY IMPACTFUL LIFE: FROM PAIN TO PURPOSE

The air smells of fear.

But I had no choice.

My fear was real.

The New York subway is no place to sleep.

And much less for a teenage girl alone.

The likelihood of a police officer waking me without compassion,

or a criminal finding me vulnerable,

left me breathless.

Every shadow seemed to hide a threat.

Every noise made me jump.

Each time the train stopped, I wondered if that would be the end.

It was 3:00 a.m.

The car was almost empty.

Only a few hopeless faces… and me.

A survivor, wide-eyed with fear.

I sat in the middle car.

It seemed safer there.

I wasn't sure...

but I needed to believe it.

That day I had boarded at the East Tremont station in the Bronx.

I knew every crossing, every street...

not because they were my home,

but because they had become my daily battlefield.

I took a train headed toward Brooklyn.

And I didn't get off.

The train reached the end of the line, changed direction...

and I stayed.

No destination.

No plan.

But clinging to the hope of not disappearing.

I didn't know where to go.

I didn't know how I'd survive another night.

But I knew I had to.

Because even though the world was dark... I still carried a small spark.

And that spark, though small... was supernatural.

And Yet, Morning Came

After hours of darkness,

of fear,

of silent tears in that subway car...

the sky began to lighten.

It wasn't sudden.

It wasn't golden rays or clear skies.

It was a timid, gray light that barely filtered through the subway windows.

But to me... it was a miracle.

My numb body couldn't take it anymore.

I had spent the night awake, eyes open, heart trembling.

Jumping at every sound, every step, every strange glance.

And yet, there I was.

Still alive.

Still standing.

Still believing.

The train kept going from station to station,

while the world outside began to wake up.

I watched it all through the window:

The first people stepping out with coffee mugs.

Cars piling into traffic.

Store lights flickering on, one by one.

New York didn't stop.

And neither did I.

I clutched my blue backpack against my chest, as if it were my armor.

I was cold.

Hungry.

MY IMPACTFUL LIFE: FROM PAIN TO PURPOSE

Exhausted.

But I also carried a deep certainty:

I had survived another night.

And if the sun had risen over me once more,

then that meant God still had me on His agenda.

I got off the train at some random station.

It wasn't a familiar or special place.

But simply stepping onto the sidewalk and feeling the fresh air on my face made me close my eyes and whisper:

—Thank You, Lord. Despite it all… morning came.

My clothes were still damp.

My shoes full of grime.

My hands frozen.

But my soul… was beginning to warm again.

Sometimes, we don't need great miracles.

Sometimes, the miracle is simply opening our eyes and seeing the light of day.

That sunrise didn't bring answers.

But it brought hope.

And in that moment... that was enough.

Surrounded by People, Alone in the World

The streets were already full.

The Bronx pulsed with its usual rhythm:

hurried people,

cars honking,

shops opening their doors.

Everything moved.

Everything carried on.

But for me... it was as if no one existed.

I walked among the crowds, yet felt like a ghost.

No one knew me.

No one spoke to me.

MY IMPACTFUL LIFE: FROM PAIN TO PURPOSE

No one noticed the skinny teenage girl

with a blue backpack hanging from her shoulder

and a deep sadness in her eyes.

I could be in the middle of the noise,

but inside me, there was a deafening silence.

It was like being in a world that didn't belong to me.

A world that ignored me.

A world that kept turning… while I stood still.

My mind kept repeating one phrase:

I need a job.

It was my constant thought.

My ongoing prayer.

My cry to heaven.

I had been searching for weeks:

knocking on doors,

asking in stores, scanning job ads.

Nothing.

Always the same answers:

—"You're too young."

—"We're not hiring."

—"You need papers."

Sometimes they didn't even bother to respond.

They just looked at me with pity... or worse, indifference.

The rejection hurt.

But more than that, it hurt to feel purposeless.

To feel useless.

To be alive... but without direction.

I sat on random benches, unfolded the subway map,

and tried to trace imaginary routes,

as if somewhere on that paper I could find a path to something better.

My eyes filled with tears.

Not because I was weak.

But because I was tired.

Tired of pretending I was fine.

Tired of waiting for a miracle that didn't come.

Tired of smiling at people, hoping someone would ask:

—"Are you okay? Do you need help?"

But no one did.

I was just another face.

Another shadow among many.

And yet... I refused to give up.

There was within me a whisper, a tiny flame that said:

Hold on. Just a little longer.

Because even if no one else knew me...

God knew exactly who I was.

The Modeling Trap

The days dragged heavily, as if time itself were playing against me.

Hunger, despair, the emptiness of not finding a job... all pushed me closer to the edge of an invisible abyss.

Every morning I sat with the same ritual: an old newspaper in my hands, scanning the classified ads for any open door.

Any door.

And then... I saw it.

"Job Opportunity for Modeling. No Experience Needed."

My eyes stopped.

My heart gave a small leap.

It seemed too good to be true.

But desperation can be a silent enemy...

and that day, it whispered in my ear:

Try it. You have nothing to lose.

I picked up the public phone.

My hands trembled as I dialed the number.

On the other end, a man's voice sounded warm, almost too friendly:

—"Of course, come. We're looking for girls like you. I'll expect you today."

He gave me the address of an old building in the Bronx, without many details.

—"It's on the fifth floor, no elevator. Just go up and knock on door 5B," he added.

I hung up with a knot in my stomach.

Something didn't feel right.

But my thoughts kept repeating:

It's an opportunity. Maybe this is the start of your way out.

I arrived in front of the building.

It was old, dark, with cracked walls and windows that looked as if they had been sealed for years.

The iron gate creaked as I pushed it.

Inside, the echo of my footsteps bounced through the empty stairwell.

Each step grew heavier as I climbed.

Second floor. Third. Fourth. Finally, the fifth.

My breathing was labored when I knocked.

A man opened.

About forty, dark hair, thick beard, and a smile far too wide.

—"Come in, please. I was waiting for you," he said in a soft voice, as if trying to lull my instincts to sleep.

I entered.

The place was a small studio, dimly lit.

A chair, a desk with scattered papers, and a large mirror covered by a dark curtain.

The air smelled of dampness, as if the walls were hiding secrets.

Nervously, I sat down.

He began to speak:

—"You're perfect... perfect for this. Slim, beautiful, model's body. You don't know how lucky you are to have called."

As he spoke, he came closer with a measuring tape.

He began taking my measurements: bust, waist, hips… legs… even attempting to measure intimate areas.

A cold chill shot down my spine.

I felt invaded. I felt the danger.

But I tried to stay calm.

Maybe this is part of the process, I told myself to keep from panicking.

And then came the next blow.

—"I need you to take off your clothes," he said, with that same unsettling smile. "It's to get your exact measurements. It's routine."

My throat closed.

My palms were sweating.

But I answered firmly:

—"That's not necessary. You can measure me over my clothes."

He hesitated.

Looked frustrated... but agreed.

Then, as if nothing had happened, he told me to wait while he went to "speak with his partner."

He left the room, closing the door behind him.

Minutes dragged on like hours.

The silence was oppressive.

My heart thundered inside my chest.

BANG!

A door slammed somewhere in the hallway.

I jumped to my feet, trembling.

Had it been a trap?

Had they locked me in?

What was happening?

A cold sweat covered my body.

My mind screamed:

Run! Get out of here!

But my feet felt nailed to the floor.

There, alone in that dark room, I closed my eyes and prayed desperately:

—"Lord... protect me. Please, don't abandon me."

And in that moment, I felt something supernatural.

A sudden calm.

A peace that descended over me, covering me like an invisible cloak.

The door swung open.

He returned, but his face had changed:

cold, calculated, direct.

—"My partner isn't interested," he said flatly.

Then... he leaned in, lowered his voice, almost conspiratorial:

—"But I have another offer for you. Not traditional modeling. It's... acting in adult films. Nothing to fear. They won't touch you. Just take off your clothes."

A knot twisted in my stomach.

My soul screamed inside.

But my face stayed calm.

Fear is cunning: it forces you to think quickly.

—"I'll think about it," I said firmly. "I'll give you my answer tomorrow."

He agreed, perhaps thinking he had me trapped.

But the moment I stepped out that door, I never looked back.

When I reached the street, the cold air hit me like an embrace of freedom.

My heart pounded wildly, but my steps were steady.

I knew I had just escaped something very dark.

Very dangerous.

Once again... God had protected me.

MY IMPACTFUL LIFE: FROM PAIN TO PURPOSE

A Shelter Called Uncertainty: When I Had to Beg for Five Cents to Eat

After so many storms, my soul longed for a breath of relief.

But there was nowhere to find it.

With the little courage I had left, I called my sister Carmen Juana collect in Santo Domingo.

Her voice, though rushed, felt like balm on the other end of the line:

—"I'll see if I can find someone to take you in, even if just for a few days," she promised, with that unconditional love only a sister knows.

She spoke with some of her husband Luis's friends, and through that desperate call, a new door opened.

I didn't know what awaited me.

I didn't know if it would be better or worse.

But at least there would be a roof.

For now.

The place: the apartment of a couple named José and Andrea.

When I arrived, the mere sight of the building made me shudder.

It was an old block, wedged between the cold streets of Brooklyn, near the New Lots station.

The train rumbled every so often, like a weary witness to the burdens carried by the souls of that neighborhood.

The façade, once white, had yellowed with time, marked by cracks like open scars.

The windows, hidden behind dirty curtains, allowed only a thread of light to slip through.

The building inspired neither trust nor comfort.

But to me, it was a roof.

A refuge… even if in the middle of uncertainty.

Inside, the thick air struck me.

It smelled of confinement, stale dampness, abandonment.

The living room was tiny.

The sofa, worn-out, stained, seams ripped, seemed to groan under the weight of the years.

A wobbly, splintered table served as the center.

MY IMPACTFUL LIFE: FROM PAIN TO PURPOSE

An old television, with a scratched screen and a collapsed antenna, completed the scene.

The kitchen was even more depressing:

a nearly empty fridge with a loose door,

a stove with broken burners,

an oven caked with hardened food,

and a cramped bathroom where mold claimed every corner.

They gave me a little room at the back, cluttered with boxes, junk, and an old mattress on the floor.

That's where I would sleep.

That's where I would try to rebuild the little that remained of my inner peace.

But reality was cruel.

Cockroaches crawled fearlessly.

Mice darted around like owners of the place.

And the air… always that heavy air of abandonment.

Andrea, the woman of the house, was not kind.

From the very beginning, she made me feel like a burden.

Her eyes were cold. Her gestures, harsh.

At first, they shared some food with me.

But soon, even that disappeared.

Words were replaced with silence.

The table with emptiness.

And then… came hunger.

My stomach roared like a wounded animal.

My legs trembled.

Weakness overcame me.

But stronger than hunger was the shame.

One afternoon, with watery eyes and a trembling voice, I went out into the street.

I walked to the New Lots train station, where the bustle hid my desperation.

I approached a public payphone, that old rusty pole I clung to like a last resort.

With my face burning in humiliation, I began to quietly ask people passing by:

MY IMPACTFUL LIFE: FROM PAIN TO PURPOSE

—"Excuse me... can you please give me 5 cents to make a phone call?"

But it wasn't to call.

It was to gather a few coins...

to buy something that would quiet the emptiness burning inside me.

I was hungry.

Every word that left my lips was a knife to my soul.

Never in my life had I begged.

Never.

I had always worked.

I had always held my dignity.

But hunger drags you to places where pride shatters.

The pain of that humiliation has no name.

Some ignored me.

Others turned their gaze away.

Some pretended not to hear.

NURISS CLARK

A few offered a coin or two.

And each time I stretched out my hand...

something inside me died a little more.

While the trains carried on their dance of iron,

I fought against pride, against despair, against the emptiness.

That day, on that forgotten platform in Brooklyn,

a fragile teenage girl with a blue backpack on her shoulder

learned what it meant to be sustained by faith alone.

Because even if everyone else ignored me...

I knew Heaven was watching.

And while I cried silently, soul shattered but head held high,

I whispered to God:

—"Lord... don't let me drown here. Move me. Lift me out of this abyss when the time is right."

Maybe nobody noticed,

but that day... I survived one more battle.

A Light in the Hallway

The days, the weeks passed...

and with them, a bit of the silence too.

In the middle of that empty routine, between the rumble of the train, the stained walls, and the contained sighs, a spark of humanity began to flicker.

The first time I saw her, I felt peace.

It was something I cannot explain with words,

as if her presence carried with it a silent promise that everything would be alright.

Her name was María.

She was a Puerto Rican neighbor, with a kind face, a soft voice, and eyes that knew how to look beyond appearances.

Her sweet accent, carried by the waves of the Caribbean,

had a way of caressing my soul—especially when she asked:

—"Nena, are you okay? I always see you so alone..."

Her words made me lower my gaze. My voice trembled. I couldn't answer.

But she didn't press further. She didn't need to.

She simply approached with a warm smile and said:

—"Come, I have a little food. Bendito... if you're hungry, eat, nena."

And that's how it began.

A plate one day.

A piece of bread the next.

Sometimes rice and beans, sometimes just coffee with toast.

But what nourished me the most...

was her gesture.

Her heart.

Her way of looking at me as if I mattered.

We didn't speak much at first.

But she always ended our brief conversations with the same phrase:

—"God bless you, nena. And don't worry... there's always a way out."

MY IMPACTFUL LIFE: FROM PAIN TO PURPOSE

One day, while I washed her dishes as a way to thank her for the food,

María looked at me and said:

—"You know, at the factory where I work, they're looking for someone. Someone to pack bottles. They don't pay much, but it's something. If you want, I'll take you tomorrow."

My eyes widened as if she had just announced a miracle.

A door.

A hope.

—"Yes, please!" —I replied, almost unable to hold back the tears.

That night, I could hardly sleep.

I lay down with my heart racing, as if life itself was finally coming back to me.

It wasn't the job of my dreams.

But it was a job. It was dignity.

It was an opportunity I would not waste.

And it was all thanks to her.

That simple woman, that neighbor who became a light in the middle of so much darkness.

The next morning, with a borrowed coat and nerves tightening my chest,

I went with María to the office where they were hiring for the factory.

The building had a cold, gray air, as if it already knew that those who walked through its doors carried broken souls but living hope.

When they called me in for the interview, the manager looked me up and down.

I could barely hold his gaze. I drew strength from my faith and said:

—"I know you'll ask me for papers... could you give me a few hours? I promise I'll bring the documents soon. I just need an opportunity."

I don't know if it was my trembling voice, my eyes full of truth,

or simply God's hand touching his heart, but the man looked at me for a few seconds in silence...

and then slowly said:

MY IMPACTFUL LIFE: FROM PAIN TO PURPOSE

—"Alright. You can start after school. Bring me the papers when you have them."

I felt as if the world was turning again for me.

As if the train of hope had finally stopped at my station.

My task was simple:

pick up bottles falling from the machine and place them into boxes, keeping up with the rhythm.

The noise was constant.

The atmosphere, cold.

The smell of freshly molded plastic filled the air every afternoon.

My hands grew sore and marked.

My body ached when I got home.

But inside...

there was a silent smile:

at last, I could earn something on my own.

When I received my first paycheck, I didn't hesitate.

The first money I earned went to pay a moral debt.

I went and handed Dolores the exact money for the ticket to New York she had bought for me.

No matter what the letter had said.

I knew what was right.

That day, when I handed over the exact amount, I didn't just settle a debt…

I also paid with gratitude.

With dignity.

With honor.

Because when one fulfills their promises,

even if the world has forgotten them…

God never forgets.

When the Factory Became a Refuge

The little stability I had managed to find began to crumble again when Andrea, the woman I had been staying with, looked at me one afternoon with a cold expression and said:

—"You can't stay here anymore."

That phrase landed like a sharp blow to the chest. There were no explanations, no gesture of comfort. Only the certainty that, once again, I was without a roof over my head.

I stayed silent. There was no room left for tears—only for decisions.

I remembered that the factory manager had a certain regard for me, maybe because of my dedication or the punctuality with which I did every task. Gathering courage, I approached him and said:

—"Sir... I need to switch shifts. Can I work at night?"

He looked at me silently for a few seconds, as if trying to read between the lines. Then he nodded:

—"Alright. You'll start nights tomorrow."

He didn't ask why. Maybe he suspected. Maybe he knew that sometimes, there are stories one simply doesn't have the strength to tell.

And so, the factory became my refuge at night.

While others left to rest, I went in to work. Among noisy machines, bottles falling into place, boxes, and the cold silence of industry, I spent my nights. The job became routine—but also shelter.

The fluorescent lights of the night shift were harsh and constant. The atmosphere turned quieter, more tense. I could hear the hum of the machines, the sharp clinks of bottles lining up, the metallic echo of boxes being sealed. I worked nonstop, my body moving in an automatic rhythm that helped me not think too much about my reality.

During my short breaks, I would hide in a corner between cardboard boxes, close my eyes, and whisper in my thoughts:

—"Lord, be my shelter tonight."

When the shift ended at dawn, I stepped out into the cold streets not knowing where to go. My little blue backpack was my faithful companion. I boarded trains with no destination and got off at random stations, just to kill time. I sat on benches, looked out the window, dozed off at times, and prayed.

I waited for the hours to pass… until night came again, so I could return to the factory.

I had no house. I had no bed. What I had was a routine that kept me alive—and a faith that, though wounded, never died.

But like all uncertain seasons, that one also came to an end.

After some time, the manager called me into his office

again. He asked about the documents I had promised to bring. I lowered my gaze. I had no way to justify my presence there anymore. I couldn't continue without a work permit.

With a heavy heart and empty hands, I was forced to leave the job. I said goodbye without complaint, without tears— just carrying the kind of sadness that stays inside and weighs like an invisible sack on your shoulders.

Before leaving, I looked one last time at the machine where I had spent so many nights. I touched the conveyor belt as if saying farewell to an old friend. In silence, I gave thanks for every day it had allowed me to survive.

And so, once again, I returned to the trains. I went back to sleeping in the subway cars that ran from Brooklyn to the Bronx, like a shadow nobody noticed. Each night was another trial: the cold, the strangers, the noises, the constant lurking danger.

But God... God was always there.

He kept me safe from puppeteers, from wicked men, from rapists, from criminals.

I had nothing. But I had His protection.

And that was enough to keep me going.

Because when the world gives you no place,

God gives you wings.

Hidden Danger Beneath a Kind Roof

One day, while speaking with my family back in Santo Domingo, they gave me the number of some people who, to my surprise, were from the same town where I was born. They lived in Brooklyn. In the middle of so much loneliness, hearing that felt like someone had lit a candle in the fog.

I remembered the husband. I had seen him at church since I was a little girl. He was familiar. And his wife, from the very first moment, showed herself to be a kind woman, generous at heart. I spoke with them over the phone, and they answered with a joyful voice that revived me:

—"Of course, young lady. Come over, we have a little room. You're welcome here."

Excitement rushed over me. After so many days wandering through trains and stations, I finally had a place where I could lay my head. I arrived at their home with my little blue backpack and a smile too big for my face. They gave me a small room all to myself. It had a bed. A roof. Peace.

At last, life seemed to be smiling at me again. The wife treated me tenderly, as if I were a long-lost daughter. I felt sheltered, cared for, human once more. Everything seemed fine... until the shadow began to move inside that home.

The husband, the very man I had known since childhood, started behaving strangely. At first, it was just little comments:

—"You're very special."

—"You deserve all that's good..."

Then came the gifts. Small details meant to disguise darker intentions. His smile grew unsettling. And when his wife left for work—since, for no apparent reason, he himself didn't work—the air in the house became heavy, charged with something unseen... but very much felt.

His stares lingered too long. His silences grew disturbing. Until one day, without pretense, he said it plainly:

—"I like you... a lot."

It felt like the ground opened beneath my feet. Suddenly, everything safe collapsed. I felt dirty, betrayed, violated. How could someone who had seen me grow up cross such a line?

But just as fear tried to paralyze me, the Spirit of God rose within me.

I withdrew. I began to lock myself in my room. I avoided any contact with him. Every step inside that house was an alert. I lived on edge, clinging to prayer, begging the Lord for a way out. Another way out.

Because that roof, which looked kind on the outside, hid a wolf in sheep's clothing.

And God, who never sleeps, began to move again.

One afternoon, I met a girl my age on the same street. Her name was Lissette. She had a mischievous smile and a sweet heart. We became friends almost without noticing. We both carried wounds, though we never confessed them fully.

I had a guitar that, ironically, had been a gift from that same man in the house. Playing a few chords helped me breathe. One day I offered Lissette:

—"If you let me borrow your birth certificate... I'll teach you to play guitar."

She agreed without hesitation. For us, it was an innocent trade: music for a paper. But for me, that document meant something far greater—the possibility of existing legally.

Of beginning again, truly. We played, laughed, strummed simple songs... and for a few hours, the world felt lighter. But when I returned to that house... hell awaited me.

The harassment worsened. His attitude grew bolder, more aggressive. Until one day, he tried to force himself on me. His body loomed menacingly, and I felt like I was breaking inside.

But then, a powerful voice burst out of me—a voice from heaven itself:

—"If you touch me, you'll go to jail! Everyone will know! Don't you dare lay a hand on me!"

I said it with authority, with a courage that only God could have given me. Inside, I trembled. But outside, I stood like a wall.

I knew I couldn't stay another second.

I grabbed my blue backpack, packed the little I had, and ran. I didn't look back. It didn't matter where I would sleep that night. I preferred the street over a house filled with shadows.

And once again, the Lord saved me. He protected me from evil.

Because when the enemy sets a trap,

God always has a way out prepared.

On the Edge of Death… The Church in Bushwick

Night fell over Brooklyn like an iron curtain.

I walked aimlessly through the streets of Bushwick, shivering with cold and fear.

I had run out of that house, and now I had nowhere to sleep.

The sky was heavy with clouds, and snowflakes began to fall.

With each step, I felt my strength slipping away.

My body was exhausted, but my soul kept searching: for shelter, a corner, something… someone… to save me.

Then I saw a dim light coming from a church.

The sign read: "Prayer Service – 7:00 PM."

I went in without thinking.

MY IMPACTFUL LIFE: FROM PAIN TO PURPOSE

There were wooden pews, old stained-glass windows, and a carpet that smelled of time itself.

I sat quietly at the back of the sanctuary, trying to disappear, as if I belonged there.

All I wanted was to rest a few minutes, to feel some human warmth, to be safe... even if only for a short while.

The service ended.

People began to leave.

No one noticed that I didn't move.

I didn't speak to anyone.

I just stayed there, still, waiting for the lights to go out.

My heart was racing, though I couldn't tell if it was from fear or from the cold.

And then it happened.

The last person shut the door.

The church fell into complete silence, as if it swallowed every sound.

The lights went out one by one.

Even the hum of the heater ceased.

And the cold... the cold began to take over, seeping through every crack, every corner.

I hid inside a closet, hugging my knees, trembling.

I had no proper coat, just the clothes of the day.

The temperature fell below zero.

The air was so frigid it stabbed at my skin like a thousand needles.

Every second was agony, a test of endurance for my body.

My hands froze stiff.

My ears burned like fire.

My feet turned to stone.

I could hardly move anymore.

The cold was winning.

I felt the blood rushing to my head.

My heartbeat slowed so much I was afraid to close my eyes.

I curled into myself, trying to create warmth with my own body, but it was useless.

MY IMPACTFUL LIFE: FROM PAIN TO PURPOSE

The wind howled outside.

Snow fell harder.

Inside, the silence was terrifying.

I couldn't even see my own hands.

It was like being buried alive in ice.

As if death itself was embracing me.

I tried to pray, but my lips trembled too much.

I felt paralyzed by the cold, as if I were slowly shutting down.

Images began flashing through my mind—my family, the sun of Santo Domingo, the smell of morning coffee... everything I had left behind.

The pain of the cold was so deep, I couldn't even cry.

I thought of my mother, my siblings, the warmth of home.

I wanted to scream, but the breath caught in my throat.

I felt trapped, powerless, condemned to die where no one would ever know I had been.

No one.

No one knew I was hiding in that church.

And then, just as my soul began to surrender, my cry reached heaven:

—"Lord, take me out of this cold! Don't let me die here!"

And like a sudden flame in the darkest night, He came to me.

I cannot explain it in words, but I felt His presence.

It was as if an invisible blanket covered me.

The cold was still there, but inside me something ignited: peace, hope, life.

It was as if a heavenly hand whispered:

—"Hold on, daughter. Morning is coming."

I didn't die that night.

I didn't freeze.

The Lord held me with His invisible hand.

And once again, when everything seemed lost, God showed me that He never abandons His children.

Slowly, the darkness began to retreat.

A faint light filtered through the church windows.

The night had passed.

I had survived.

I felt I had defeated death itself.

My legs, numb, barely responded.

With effort, I stood.

My bones cracked like dry branches.

My fingers were purple.

My clothes damp from the icy breath of the night.

And yet, with every step toward the door, I felt life returning.

As if I were being reborn from the depths of the abyss.

I pushed open the heavy door and stepped outside.

The sky, once dark and threatening, was painted with shades of pink and orange.

The sun was rising, as if heaven itself embraced me.

The first rays of dawn kissed my frozen face.

The air was still cold, but now it was no longer my enemy.

Now it was proof that I was alive.

My feet, sore and clumsy, walked along the sidewalk as the city awakened.

Snow crunched beneath my steps.

Life, little by little, returned.

I left the church as though I had been born again.

As I walked through the streets of Brooklyn, the sun lit the buildings and sidewalks in golden hues.

My body, which had teetered on the edge of hypothermia hours before, began to recover its warmth.

Blood coursed through my veins like a thawing river.

A powerful Presence had rescued me from the cruelty of that winter night.

I thought I would become a statistic… or worse, a tragic headline:

"Teenager freezes to death in empty Brooklyn church."

I thought I would be one of those forgotten stories.

But God had other plans.

The world regained its colors, and I, humbled and grateful, walked without a roof, without food, without work...

but certain that this would not be the last day of my life.

It was the beginning of something new.

I had lived through the longest night of my existence.

And now the sun bore witness that I was still standing.

People rushed past me, indifferent, unaware.

No one knew what I had just endured.

No one imagined that this frail young girl, with wrinkled clothes and slow steps, had just been delivered from death.

But I knew. And God knew.

I had been born again.

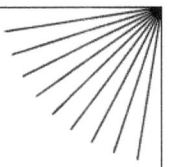

CHAPTER 7

**Puerto Rico The Process
That Shaped My Character
Hard times, the room without a bed,
arrest, injustice, betrayals**

My body could no longer take it. I was exhausted. My soul was heavy, and my heart had grown a little harder, like a shield against so much pain. I had endured hunger, cold, rejection, abuse, and abandonment. I had slept in trains, cried in stations, prayed in hidden corners. I had clung to my faith with the few forces left that kept me standing.

And then, once again, God intervened.

I could not remain in New York any longer. That cycle had ended. I felt it in the air, in my steps, deep within my soul. And so, without many explanations, another door opened: Puerto Rico.

The decision wasn't planned; it was guidance to enter another process. Something within me told me this was the next destination, even though I had no idea what awaited me there. But by then, I had stopped asking too many questions. I had learned to walk by faith and not by sight. I knew the Lord had not brought me this far to abandon me halfway.

With the little I had, I took a flight to that Caribbean island, carrying a wounded heart but a hope that still beat strong. The plane took off from New York, leaving behind not just a city, but a chapter filled with scars, miracles, and lessons.

Puerto Rico awaited me. Not with flowers or open arms, but with a new process that would also mark my history. There, too, I would have to fight, survive, and start again.

It was another desert. But also, another opportunity to witness the hand of God at work.

Puerto Rico received me with a different kind of sun, with new streets and a familiar language that somehow sounded different. It was another world inside the same tongue. And yet, the loneliness hadn't left me; it had simply changed its scenery.

One afternoon, after wandering through streets with my blue backpack on my shoulder—carrying more hope than belongings—I arrived at a church in Santurce. It was Sunday. Though I had come early, the service wouldn't begin until evening. I sat on one of the pews, gazing at the windows, listening to the echo of my thoughts as the sun leaned toward the horizon.

I waited there all afternoon. No one knew I was alone. No one imagined I had no place to sleep. But I knew God knew. And that was enough.

Little by little, the lights came on. Brothers and sisters from the congregation began to arrive, greeting one another, preparing for the service. Then, a couple caught my attention: he was much older, with gray hair and a calm gaze. She was young, full of energy. They approached me with a sincere smile.

"Hi, God bless you. When did you arrive? Where are you from?"

I told them I had just arrived in Puerto Rico and had nowhere to stay. They looked at me, then at each other, and without hesitation, the woman exclaimed:

—"What?! That's no problem. You're coming with us. Tonight, you'll stay at our house."

I froze. I couldn't believe it. Once again, God used strangers to extend a hand to me exactly when I needed it most.

That night, they took me to their home. A modest place, but filled with peace. They offered me food, a roof, and above all, words of comfort. I felt God's presence had led me to that pew, to that moment, to those people.

As we grew closer, they told me about a woman from the church—a Dominican sister who had started her own small business. They said perhaps she could give me work.

—"She also came from there. She'll understand. Tomorrow, we'll speak to her," they assured me.

And so, as night fell in a strange land, heaven opened another door.

Because when you think everything is lost... God is already preparing the next chapter.

An Unexpected Beginning

That very same week, the couple who had opened the doors of their home to me took me to meet the Dominican woman from the church. She was a woman with a strong character, sharp eyes, and a firm voice—but with a heart that, surprisingly, knew how to open when it came to helping others. She welcomed me into her home as someone who opens not only a door, but an entirely new stage of life.

The first thing she asked me was:

—"What's your name?"

And without thinking much, I replied:

—"Call me Lissette."

It wasn't my real name, but it was the name of a little friend

I had met in New York. A sweet girl with whom I had shared afternoons of guitar, innocent laughter, and a tiny fragment of hope. I liked that name. It sounded like a new beginning. Like a version of me that could be born without the weight of scars.

The woman nodded in agreement and said, without hesitation:

—"Alright, Lissette, I'm going to help you. But you're going to work as well."

She spoke of a property she owned nearby—a kind of boarding house she had divided into several small rooms, which she rented to people in need. Each room had access to shared bathrooms, and the atmosphere was... tense. Not warm, not cozy, but functional. It was shelter.

We walked there together. The building seemed worn out from the passing of time. The walls were faded. The doors, rusted and creaking. When we arrived, she opened one of the doors and said:

—"This is what you're going to do. Clean the bathrooms, sweep, mop. Keep everything in order."

I stood in silence, feeling a knot tightening in my throat.

I had never done that before.

I had never cleaned a bathroom. I didn't know how to sweep properly. In my childhood, no one had taught me household chores. It wasn't pride—it was simply ignorance.

I looked down at my trembling hands. The smell of bleach and disinfectant struck me like a slap of reality. Then she placed in my hands a bucket, a brush, a rag, and a gallon of bleach.

I didn't say a word. I simply nodded and swallowed hard.

I knew this was the door that had opened before me.

It wasn't the prettiest one. It wasn't the easiest.

But it was the one God had placed in front of me.

And if He had opened it...

He would also teach me how to walk through it.

The Weight of the First Day

That first day of work at the boarding house felt like a direct blow to the soul.

The sun had barely begun to rise timidly above the rooftops, and there I was—bucket in hand, kneeling on the icy floor of a bathroom that seemed to have been forgotten by cleanliness for centuries. The stench of bleach, dampness, and stale air struck me like a violent wave, making my head pound and my stomach churn. But there I was. Willing to learn. To obey. To begin, even if it hurt.

The instructions were clear.

What wasn't clear was how I was supposed to endure.

My body was not prepared.

I had never scrubbed a toilet, never scraped grime from walls, never mopped such endless stretches of dirty concrete hallways.

Every movement felt like a battle.

My hands, once soft and inexperienced, began to split into burning cracks. The bleach scorched my skin mercilessly. My knees ached as if they had endured years of blows against the floor. My joints creaked like brittle branches breaking apart. And my feet... my poor feet... felt the weight of the day as if they carried stones.

The hours dragged on, and it seemed like nothing improved.

I would clean one bathroom... and another would already be in ruins.

I would sweep the hallway... and the dust would creep

back in, mocking me, as though the very filth refused to be defeated.

The stares of some tenants were intimidating.

Their whispers cut like invisible knives against my dignity.

But I did not lift my gaze. I was not seeking pity or compassion.

I only wanted to fulfill my duty. To honor the Dominican woman who had taken me in.

And above all... I wanted to honor God, who was silently holding me together while my strength crumbled drop by drop.

By the time evening came, when the last corner had been scrubbed, I felt I would collapse.

My body refused to respond.

I sank onto an old rag in a hidden corner, hugged my legs tightly, and tried to contain the trembling within me.

My hands burned.

My feet were like blocks of stone.

Every bone inside me seemed to groan in silence.

And yet…

I felt alive.

Because I was fighting.

Because I had not given up.

Because while everything in me screamed "enough"…

I had said, "Here I am."

That day, I did not just clean a bathroom.

That day, I began to cleanse myself within.

To tear despair out by the root.

To rebuild myself from the simplest, from the lowest, from the most sacred place.

That was…

the weight of the first day.

And also, the weight of my rebirth.

Rebeca and the Trap of Trust

The first days in Rebeca's house were easier than I imagined.

She appeared kind. Almost maternal.

She offered me coffee in the mornings, asked me how I had slept, sat with me while I rested after hours of cleaning. Her words, at first, were as sweet as honey.

—"I was lost," she told me one day, her eyes glistening, "but God rescued me. And now, here I am, with a family I never dreamed of having."

Her confessions moved me deeply.

They made me lower my guard.

I thought: *"Maybe this woman really does know what it means to come from nothing... what it means to rise from the ashes."*

And so, I began to trust. I began to feel that maybe I wasn't so alone. That this woman had been sent by God in the middle of my desert.

But, with time, her sweetness began to taste like manipulation.

Her words no longer just lifted my spirit... they silently wove a web of dependency.

MY IMPACTFUL LIFE: FROM PAIN TO PURPOSE

She made me feel as if I owed her something.

As if that roof, that food, and that place where I worked until I was breathless… were gifts I could never question.

She gave me heavier and heavier responsibilities.

More hours. More bathrooms. More effort.

But she disguised it as opportunity, as if she were doing me a favor.

—"Look how the Lord opened this door for you, Lissette," she would say, with a smile as kind as it was controlling. "Here you are safe, you have a roof, food… and you're even learning a trade. Be thankful, because not everyone is as good as I am."

Each phrase was an invisible rope tightening around my soul.

Each time she smiled, I felt my freedom take one more step back.

It was as if she were telling me without saying it: *"Don't complain. You belong to me."*

I began to notice that, although she spoke of God and hope, not everything in her heart was light.

There were shadows hidden behind every pious word.

And that's when I understood the true meaning of her name.

Rebeca.

In Hebrew, *trap*.

And yes... she was a trap disguised as a refuge.

A woman who used the language of faith as a chain.

Who spoke of God so you wouldn't run.

Who offered shelter in order to wield power.

Who used her past to sweeten the poison.

But I didn't see it at first.

I still had more to live... more to hurt...

before I could see her true face.

And so began another process.

Another desert.

One more silent, more mental, but just as hard.

And there, once again, God would begin to sharpen my discernment.

So I could see not with my eyes... but with my spirit.

The Promised Account

Months went by, and one evening after an exhausting day cleaning the boarding house, Rebeca took me back to her home.

That night, she was especially kind... almost too kind.

She served me dinner with a serene smile—one of those smiles that blended tenderness with something I couldn't quite decipher. She looked at me as if she knew something I didn't, as if the next step had already been calculated.

"Look, Lissette," she said while I ate in silence. "Here, you're going to earn money. What you do has value. Tomorrow, I'll take you to the bank. I'm going to open an account for you so you can start saving. You can't work like this without putting something aside for the future."

Her words froze me for a moment. I didn't know what to say.

After so many months walking with empty pockets, sleeping in train stations, on hard benches with fear pressing against my chest... the thought of having my own account, my own place to keep even the little I could earn—

It felt like breathing again after being underwater too long.

"Thank you," I whispered with sincerity, my voice trembling with emotion.

"Don't worry. Trust me," she answered with that soft, calming tone of hers. "You'll be fine here. Everything will work out."

That night, I went to bed with my body aching, but with my heart just a little lighter.

There was something in the air... a sense that maybe, just maybe, things would start to change. That after such a long desert, a breeze of hope might finally come.

But I had already learned not to trust too quickly.

I had learned that, many times,

what looks like a blessing... hides a trap.

The promise of opening an account,

of giving me financial freedom,

of teaching me how to grow... did not come alone.

It carried a hidden intention.

One I could not yet see, but one I would soon understand.

All I knew was that, come morning, we would go to the bank.

And with that step... perhaps a new chapter would begin.

One more.

One more in the long journey of discovering who can truly be trusted...

and learning that not all promises come from heaven.

The Dawn of a Promise

Just as the sun began to rise over the muted sky of Santurce, Rebeca called out to me with urgency.

"Get up, Lissette. Let's go to the bank now, while they're just opening," she said in that hurried but firm tone of hers, as if she held the clock of destiny in her hands.

I dressed quickly, my heart pounding as though it already knew this day would mark a before and after.

We walked to a branch just a few blocks from her house.

The bank was simple, old, its windows lined with dust, the rhythmic tapping of typewriter keys filling the air like a mechanical heartbeat.

We sat down in front of a desk.

A bank clerk welcomed us with a kind smile.

But it was Rebeca who spoke for me.

She explained that I was young, that I had just started working with her, and that she wanted to help me open an account so I could save the little I earned.

I barely said a word.

I simply nodded.

I didn't understand banks or paperwork.

But I trusted.

I trusted the voices guiding me.

I trusted Rebeca's firm tone, which carried itself with such natural authority.

A few moments later, I signed the documents.

And they handed me a small passbook with my name on it.

MY IMPACTFUL LIFE: FROM PAIN TO PURPOSE

My name.

Rebeca looked at me with a smile that, at that moment, felt sincere.

"Look, now you have your own account. From now on, everything you earn goes here. That's progress, Lissette," she said, as if she were handing me the keys to a brand-new future.

I held the passbook with both hands.

I clutched it as if it were a treasure.

As if inside it I could store all the dignity the world had denied me.

For an instant... I felt like something in my life was finally beginning to align.

But what I didn't know was that not every door others open leads to freedom.

And not everything that shines comes from God.

Because even though the account bore my name...

not everything placed in it would truly belong to me.

That morning brought a promise.

But it also carried... a silent warning.

The Price of Staying

I stayed.

Not because I wanted to,

but because I had nowhere else to go.

That boarding house, with its smell of disinfectant mixed with dampness and resignation, was the only place where I could sleep without fear... though never without pain.

Every morning, without fail, I rose before the sun.

I picked up the bucket, the rags, the jug of bleach,

and began the routine.

Scrub. Wash. Wipe. Start again.

As if my entire life had been reduced to that:

erasing the dirt of others... while mine kept piling up inside.

At first, Rebeca seemed cordial.

But it didn't take long for her to show another face.

The shouting began.

The scolding.

MY IMPACTFUL LIFE: FROM PAIN TO PURPOSE

The humiliations.

"That's wrong! Don't you know how to clean? Do it again! Don't waste my time!"

Her harsh words ripped through me.

And I lowered my head.

I didn't even have the strength to defend myself.

Everything hurt:

My hands, cracked and raw from the bleach.

My feet, swollen as if they carried the weight of the world.

My knees, my wrists, my shoulders…

every part of me was a silent scream.

But what hurt most was the contempt.

The feeling of being invisible.

The sense that, to her, I wasn't a person,

just a tool.

I tried to do well.

I pushed myself harder.

I repeated the tasks over and over,

scrubbing until my body gave out.

But for Rebeca, it was never enough.

She always found something wrong.

She always found a way to make me feel clumsy, useless… unworthy.

And I… I was just a girl.

A teenager with no experience, no training, no one to teach me.

I learned through tears and rebukes.

I learned under the weight of her shouting.

And yet, I stayed.

Because Rebeca paid me.

Little, yes. But something.

And with that "something," I saved every cent in that bank account.

I never touched the money.

I guarded it like a sacred secret.

Because to me, that little passbook wasn't just paper and numbers.

It was a plan.

A ray of hope.

I pretended I was fine.

I smiled when I had to.

But deep inside, I knew that place was not a home.

It was a shelter with an expiration date.

A stopover in the middle of my storm.

I endured.

I kept quiet.

I obeyed.

But inside me...

something was awakening.

And though no one else could see it,

I knew:

I would not stay there forever.

Screams in the Boarding House

The days went by…

and I was still there.

Waking up very early, walking to Rebeca's property with a body aching and eyes swollen from accumulated exhaustion.

I grabbed my bucket, the rags, the jug of bleach, and began the day's work.

These weren't simple tasks.

I had to scrub bathrooms used by strangers, mop floors that never seemed clean, carry buckets of water with trembling arms.

And I was just a girl.

A teenager forced to grow up too soon.

One who came from another world,

a world where adult responsibility was still a mystery.

But there was no time for innocence anymore.

Here there was only work.

Exhaustion.

MY IMPACTFUL LIFE: FROM PAIN TO PURPOSE

And screams.

Rebeca, who had once shown kindness,

began to change.

"That's not how it's done!"

"Don't you know how to do anything?"

"Do it again! Clean it all over again!"

Her voice cracked like a whip down the hallway.

And every word was a blow—

one that left no visible marks,

but carved deep wounds inside me.

She shouted in front of others,

as if I had no value,

as if I were just an object that failed again and again.

I lowered my head.

Not out of submission,

but out of exhaustion.

Because I no longer had the strength to explain what no one understood:

that no one had ever taught me how to scrub floors,

how to make bathrooms shine,

how to polish everything until it "sparkled" the way she demanded.

My hands cracked open in painful fissures.

My fingers turned red, stiff.

Every joint ached, as if my body were aging all at once.

And at night, I lay down with a broken soul.

But the next morning,

I got up again.

Not because it didn't hurt.

But because I had no other choice.

I stayed because Rebeca paid me.

Little, yes. Very little.

But I saved it all.

MY IMPACTFUL LIFE: FROM PAIN TO PURPOSE

Every single dollar, I treasured like a hidden diamond.

I never touched that money.

It was my hope.

My silent plan.

My invisible ticket to another life.

I stayed with her for a while.

Because I had nowhere else to go.

Because that house, though cold, still had a roof.

Because that voice, though harsh, came with the little pay that kept my secret dreams alive.

I didn't know how much longer I could endure.

But I knew one thing…

I would not give up.

And though her screams tried to break me on the outside,

something inside me was slowly growing stronger.

The Unjust Arrest

It was Saturday.

And I woke up with a knot in my chest.

A thick sadness wrapped around me like a damp blanket.

That day, nostalgia consumed me.

I missed my mother, my father, the laughter of my siblings.

My throat was tight, my soul tender, my heart fragile.

That day I got paid.

It wasn't much, but it was mine.

The fruit of my cracked hands.

Of my swollen feet.

Of my silent dawns soaked in bleach and fatigue.

It was the quiet reward of pressing on, without applause.

I walked to the bank, eyes still damp.

I was going to deposit the little I had, as always.

It was my sacred routine.

MY IMPACTFUL LIFE: FROM PAIN TO PURPOSE

My small act of faith.

The sun burned brightly over Santurce.

But inside me... everything was clouded.

I waited in line.

Envelope in hand.

I watched people talking, laughing, making plans.

All I wanted was to save that money.

My small achievement.

My seed.

And then...

the world stopped.

Two policemen walked in.

Their steps cut through the air.

They looked at me. Straight. Without hesitation.

One of them spoke with a voice of stone:

"You. Come with us."

I froze.

"What's going on?" I asked, trembling.

"Why are you arresting me? I haven't done anything!"

My heart pounded furiously against my chest.

One of them snatched the envelope from my hands.

Just like that. Without care. Without compassion.

"For this money," he said.

I felt stripped.

Exposed.

Ashamed.

As if my dignity had been thrown to the ground.

"That money is mine! I worked for it! I got paid today! I haven't stolen anything!" I cried, my voice breaking with tears.

But they didn't listen.

They didn't want to listen.

They didn't want to see the trembling girl in front of them.

MY IMPACTFUL LIFE: FROM PAIN TO PURPOSE

They only saw the envelope.

They only saw suspicion.

They didn't see my scars.

They didn't see my sleepless nights.

They didn't see my story.

They put handcuffs on me.

Right there.

In public.

As if I were a criminal.

As if my life had no value.

As if I were nothing.

People stared.

Some whispered.

Others turned away.

I stood there, exposed, humiliated, broken.

Tears streamed down my face.

My heart shattered into pieces.

My hands... empty.

In my mind, only one cry echoed:

"My God, don't let this happen!"

Where was justice?

Where was respect for a girl who only wanted to survive?

They took me away.

And the money...

the fruit of my tears, of my worn-out knees...

remained with them.

In that moment, something inside me broke.

But also, something ignited.

Because even if the world turned its back on me...

I knew God never would.

Because I knew who I was.

And so did He.

Pointed Out in the Crowd

Just when I thought it couldn't get any worse...

she appeared among the crowd.

Rebeca.

The woman who had given me a roof.

The one who said God had rescued her.

The one who yelled at me for not making the bathrooms shine.

The one who spoke of faith while binding me with fear.

Now...

she pointed her finger at me.

Her eyes filled with fury.

Her voice dripping with poison.

Shouting so everyone could hear:

"That's her! That girl is a thief! She stole that money from me!"

And my world... collapsed.

I couldn't understand.

I couldn't react.

Everything turned blurry.

"That's not true! That money was what you paid me for cleaning your property!"

I shouted, my voice breaking, my soul trembling.

But no one listened.

The police—

without checking,

without investigating,

without a doubt—

simply repeated:

"Let's go. You stole it."

"I didn't steal anything! I earned it working!" I begged.

But it was like shouting underwater.

As if my words had no value.

MY IMPACTFUL LIFE: FROM PAIN TO PURPOSE

As if I had no value.

They handcuffed me right there.

In the middle of the bank.

In front of everyone.

My wrists burned.

My face burned with shame.

And my heart… collapsed inside my chest.

Everyone believed I was guilty just because she said so.

Rebeca kept yelling,

each word stabbing me like a knife:

"Take her away! I picked her up off the street and this is how she repays me—by stealing from me!"

"That's a lie!" I managed to whisper, my tears mixing with rage.

"You know that's not true!"

But no one defended me.

No one.

They shoved me.

My feet barely moved.

The cuffs cut into my skin,

but what hurt the most…

was the silence of the innocent.

They dragged me through the street, handcuffed,

while the crowd followed.

Some whispered.

Others laughed.

And I just cried.

A child.

Hands bound.

Soul shattered.

Falsely accused.

Exposed as if I were a monster.

I didn't know whether to scream or stay silent.

To run or surrender.

But inside me, as I dragged my feet,

as stares pierced me like knives,

one phrase repeated like a warm breath:

"God knows the truth."

How to Carry the Cross

They dragged me through the street...

handcuffed.

As if I were a criminal.

As if the weight of a lie could erase my truth.

My feet stumbled.

My breath grew short.

Shame suffocated me.

But the cruelest part...

was not the handcuffs.

Not the shoves.

Not the policemen's shouts.

It was the crowd.

That crowd who didn't know me,

who didn't know my story,

who had never seen my knees pressed against the floor in prayer

or my cracked hands bleeding from work.

Yet they followed me…

as if I were a spectacle.

All of them staring.

With those eyes that don't ask,

that don't doubt,

that only judge.

And I wept.

I wept like never before.

With a wound that did not bleed on the outside…

but tore me apart on the inside.

I cried out with a voice broken into pieces:

"Please! I didn't do anything! Let me go! Set me free!"

But it was like shouting into a storm.

My words vanished into the wind.

No one heard me.

And then...

in the middle of that hell,

an image filled my mind:

Jesus.

Carrying His cross.

Walking through the streets.

Escorted by soldiers.

Followed by a blind, mocking crowd,

hungry for scandal.

That's how I felt.

A broken child.

Dragged through the streets.

Pointed at, condemned…

yet innocent.

And though my tears did not stop,

though my body trembled,

from the deepest part of my soul

a prayer rose:

"Lord… You know I didn't steal.

You know I am innocent.

Do not abandon me."

It was the most humiliating procession of my life.

But I did not walk alone.

I knew it.

I felt it.

Someone was watching me from above.

MY IMPACTFUL LIFE: FROM PAIN TO PURPOSE

Someone was walking beside me.

Someone who had also been humiliated.

Who had also been falsely accused.

Who had also been dragged through streets He did not deserve.

Shame.

Desperation.

Pain.

All pierced me like blades.

And yet… I did not fall.

Because even handcuffed,

even surrounded by hatred,

even shattered on the outside…

I kept believing.

And that faith,

that flame…

not even the crowd, nor the injustice,

nor the humiliation,

could extinguish.

The Final Stab

By the time we reached the police station...

I had no strength left.

I was drenched in tears.

My body trembled—

not from the cold...

but from fear.

From helplessness.

From the shame of being treated like something worthless.

Like an inconvenience.

Like a mistake.

But the worst... was still to come.

Rebeca stepped forward with firm steps.

And from her purse, as if pulling out a weapon,

she drew my passport.

My identity.

My name.

My story.

My origin.

That little red booklet that said who I was

and where I came from.

And with it, she handed over my birth certificate as well.

My entire existence, condensed into two pieces of paper.

She placed them in the hands of the officers.

And with a coldness that froze me to the core, she said:

"Look… she's Dominican. She has no papers. Deport her."

It was as if someone had stabbed a knife into my chest.

And then… twisted it with contempt.

I looked at her.

Searching for a shred of mercy.

A glimpse of humanity.

But I saw no compassion.

I saw betrayal.

I saw cruelty.

I saw coldness disguised as righteousness.

"Why are you doing this?" I asked, my voice barely a whisper.

"I worked for you! I didn't steal anything! You know that!"

But she…

turned her back on me.

As if I were nothing.

As if everything I had done for her

was worth less than the air I breathed.

As if I were trash.

That was the final stab.

MY IMPACTFUL LIFE: FROM PAIN TO PURPOSE

It wasn't enough to accuse me.

Now she wanted to erase me.

Expel me.

Wipe me off the map as if I had never existed.

The officers examined my papers.

They spoke in low voices among themselves.

They looked at me as if I were a problem...

not a person.

And there I was.

A teenage girl.

With no home.

No justice.

No defense.

Not a single familiar face to speak on my behalf.

On the verge of being deported...

because of the cruel words of a woman

who claimed to fear God,

but wielded her voice like a weapon.

In that moment, I could do only one thing.

The only thing left to me.

Pray.

"Lord… please… let this not be my last page.

Do not allow this to be the end."

Because deep in my soul,

I still knew it wasn't over.

I still had life to live.

Battles to win.

Stories to write.

And even if they tried to erase me…

God would not allow it.

The Room Without a Bed

They threw me into an empty room,

as if tossing away something no longer useful.

There was no bed.

No blanket.

No dignity.

Only four dirty walls,

a white light buzzing like a lament,

and an air so heavy

that even breathing felt like an act of defiance.

I sat on the floor, hugging my knees,

as if I could still shield myself from the world...

as if there was still something left that was mine.

I didn't close my eyes the entire night.

Exhaustion pressed on my body like a stone slab...

but my soul,

my soul stayed awake, broken, trembling.

Everything hurt.

But more than my body...

it hurt simply to exist like that.

In that crushing silence,

in that loneliness louder than a thousand voices,

I fell to my knees.

I didn't care if someone saw me.

I didn't care about the dirty floor.

I didn't care about anything.

I just wanted to speak with God.

My only refuge.

My only witness.

My only hope.

With my face against the floor and my voice in pieces, I prayed:

MY IMPACTFUL LIFE: FROM PAIN TO PURPOSE

"Lord...

I have no one.

They've taken my freedom, my name, my dignity...

but You know me.

You know I'm not a thief.

You saw every tear, every sleepless night,

every bathroom I scrubbed.

Have mercy on me."

And then... it happened.

It wasn't a noise.

It wasn't a human voice.

It was something that ignited inside me,

like a sacred spark,

like a whisper that shook me to my bones.

"Do not be afraid.

I will bring you out of here."

I hadn't imagined it.

It wasn't exhaustion playing tricks.

I felt it. I heard it. I knew it.

It was Him.

Speaking to me.

Holding me up.

And though I was still in that room without a bed,

though my wrists still burned from the handcuffs,

though I had no idea what was coming next…

that promise was enough.

Because if God had spoken,

then the bars didn't matter,

nor the papers they wanted to strip from me,

nor the filthy floor beneath me.

He was going to take me out of there.

And with that…

though I didn't sleep,

I finally rested.

The Justice of Heaven

The day had been long.

Endless.

The clock seemed to have stopped along with my breath.

There were still shadows circling my heart,

but inside me

burned a certainty that could not be extinguished:

—"Do not be afraid. I will bring you out of here."

And so it was.

As the sun began to set behind the buildings of Santurce,

the immigration officers arrived.

Their steps were different.

Not like those of that morning.

They did not come with shouts or chains.

They came with another spirit... with another air.

One of them called me by my name.

My real name.

Not "thief," not "suspect," not "nobody."

He called me as one who recognizes a person.

As one who looks with humanity.

They led me to a small room.

No bars.

No insults.

Only questions.

Only attention.

They interviewed me.

Reviewed documents.

Listened to me.

And for the first time in a long while,

MY IMPACTFUL LIFE: FROM PAIN TO PURPOSE

I spoke with a trembling voice, yet with unwavering truth.

I told them my story.

I told them who I was.

I spoke of the work, of my cracked hands,

of the wages that never reached my pocket,

of the false accusation,

and of the dagger disguised as help that was Rebeca.

And then... it happened.

One of them came closer.

Took my hands.

And released the handcuffs.

That metallic *click*,

that dry sound,

was heavenly music to my soul.

The officer looked into my eyes with both firmness and kindness and said:

—"You may go."

She didn't shout.

She didn't push me.

She set me free.

I felt my whole soul exhale.

As if I had been holding my breath for days.

As if I could finally breathe without fear.

But that wasn't all.

They explained that Rebeca would face consequences.

Charges for falsehood, for manipulation, for handing over documents that were not hers.

God not only set me free.

God brought justice.

Because heaven does not forget.

And when earth closes the door,

heaven opens a window with authority.

I left the station with tears clouding my eyes.

I had no home.

I didn't know where my next roof would be.

But I had something far greater:

My name.

My dignity.

My freedom.

And the absolute certainty that heaven had defended me.

I was not invisible.

I was not alone.

God had spoken.

And God had fulfilled His promise.

The Return with Dignity

As soon as I regained my freedom,

the very first thing I longed to do was return to those who had received me with love

when I first arrived in Puerto Rico:

Guillermo and Laura,

the couple from the church in Santurce

who once opened their doors to me without even knowing me,

when I had nothing.

I called them.

My voice trembled.

I told them everything.

Every tear.

Every injustice.

Every humiliation.

Every silent blow I had carried inside.

And when I finished,

what I heard on the other end of the line

made me cry again…

but this time, with relief.

"Forgive us, Nuriss...

we didn't know.

We never imagined Rebeca was like that."

They didn't just believe me.

They felt responsible.

And they acted.

With a love that could only be born from the heart of God,

Guillermo and Laura bought me a ticket back to New York.

They didn't offer it as a favor...

but as **restitution**.

As an act of divine justice.

When I held that ticket in my hand,

I looked at it as if it were a symbol from heaven.

It wasn't just a plane ticket.

It was a written declaration from God Himself:

I lifted you.

I defended you.

I restored you.

Keep walking. I am with you.

On the day of the flight,

I said goodbye to Puerto Rico with my soul split in two.

This island had seen me cry.

It had seen me fall.

It had seen me scrub bathrooms with bleeding hands.

Sleep without rest.

Fight without strength.

Be accused, humiliated, and condemned...

But it was also the place where God spoke to me.

Where He defended me.

Where certain hearts became true angels along my path.

With tears filling my eyes, I boarded the plane.

I didn't leave with resentment.

I left with lessons.

With scars, yes...

but also with a faith more resilient.

More mature.

More alive.

Because despite everything I had endured,

God was still writing my story.

And deep within my soul, I knew...

there were still many pages left to be written.

Wings Toward a New Beginning

The plane took off...

and with it, so did my thoughts.

I was flying back to New York,

but in reality,

I was returning to life itself.

The blue backpack was still the same,

but the girl carrying it...

was no longer the same.

Now she carried invisible scars,

marks from a silent war she had survived.

And also, a faith deeper,

stronger,

tested and proven.

The roar of the engines filled the air,

but my soul was quiet, reflective.

I looked out the window

and could not help but remember everything I was leaving behind:

the tears,

the betrayal,

the cell without a bed...

But also, the voice that had whispered to me:

Do not be afraid.

I arrived at the New York airport

with my heart pounding hard.

I didn't know what awaited me,

but I knew God was already there, waiting.

From Santo Domingo,

my parents had done everything they could

to help me find a new refuge.

They had spoken with Pedro,

a brother from my father's church,

who had family in New York.

And that was how I found myself

in the arms of **Tino and his wife, Ruthy.**

They received me as if they had always known me,

as if they understood that I wasn't just arriving with a bag, but with a story that deserved a new beginning.

Their faces radiated peace.

Their home, though humble,

held something I had been missing so deeply:

human warmth.

"Welcome, my daughter.

This is your home," Ruthy told me with a smile

that broke me inside… but with relief.

I didn't need luxury.

I just needed a place

where no one would shout at me,

where I could sleep without fear,

where I could begin to heal.

And I found it.

God had kept His word…

once again.

CHAPTER 8

The Refuge That Healed My Wounds, New Connections

The first time I set foot in Tino and Ruthy's house in Queens,

I found myself in a space of deep tranquility...

It wasn't just a house... it was a refuge.

A soft lamp poured its light over the walls, draped in warm shadows,

floral curtains swayed gently with the breeze,

and the air carried something I hadn't felt in so long:

the smell of home.

Of freshly cooked food.

Of hope simmered with love and patience.

I stood still, speechless,

absorbing that sensation I had longed for so desperately: **safety.**

Tino, a Dominican with an open heart and a sunlit smile,

shook my hand with such strength

that it felt as though he was gathering the broken pieces of my soul

and helping me become whole again.

—"This is your home now, my girl!" he said,

and his laughter was like a cascade of relief that filled the entire room.

Behind him stood Ruthy, his Puerto Rican wife,

with that gentleness that could pierce through any wall.

She looked at me as if she had known me forever.

—"Come, sit down... you must be hungry," she said.

Then I saw the table.

A feast that seemed like it had descended from a divine celebration:

rice, beans, meat, sweet plantains...

but the most powerful thing wasn't the food,

it was the gesture.

No one had ever awaited me like that.

No one had ever welcomed me that way.

Not as a burden... but as someone sent from heaven.

Their children were also at the table,

small, curious, tender.

Their eyes didn't judge.

Their eyes said: *"you're safe."*

And as I ate, my tears blended with the flavors.

Not because of sadness.

But because of the overwhelming emotion of feeling,

for the first time in so long...

that I was truly safe.

—"Welcome to our home, Nuriss."

Ruthy's voice was like a lullaby.

Soft. Sincere. Gentle.

And then she hugged me.

Without haste.

Without formality.

Just with her soul.

At first, I froze, surprised.

I wasn't used to gestures like that.

My body hesitated…

but my soul needed it so much,

that in seconds, my arms lifted on their own…

and I hugged her back.

In that instant, something inside me broke.

And at the same time… began to heal.

A *"welcome"* and a hug from a woman who didn't even know me…

returned to me the part of my soul I thought I had lost.

After the train stations, the sleepless nights, the deceptions,

and that cell without a bed…

that moment was a flame lit in the middle of the ice.

MY IMPACTFUL LIFE: FROM PAIN TO PURPOSE

There I was,

in a stranger's home,

thousands of miles away from my parents, my homeland, my childhood...

And for the first time in a very long time,

I didn't feel alone.

The walls of that house weren't luxurious.

But the people who lived inside...

were immensely rich.

Rich in kindness.

In faith.

In compassion.

And I, carrying more scars than belongings,

began to feel something I thought I had lost: **hope.**

Days of Peace, Prayer, and Reunions

Days turned into weeks.

And weeks, into months.

Without realizing it, my soul began to breathe slower, deeper, more peacefully.

I lived with Tino and Ruthy as if I were part of their family.

I studied with effort.

I worked with dignity.

And every Sunday, our mornings began with more than breakfast: they began with prayer.

Before heading to Bay Ridge Christian Center,

we would sit at the table—with steaming cups of coffee and toasted bread—

and join our hands, our voices, and our hearts.

—"Lord, thank You for Your provision. Thank You for this roof. And thank You for Nuriss's new beginning."

That's how Tino prayed, always with his soul in every word.

And while we prayed,

MY IMPACTFUL LIFE: FROM PAIN TO PURPOSE

I cried silently,

because I knew I was witnessing the fulfillment

of promises that had once only been whispers in the cold.

But the greatest surprise came one ordinary Sunday,

as we were leaving the church,

when I heard a voice that shook me to my core:

—"Nuriss!"

It was a familiar voice... with the accent of my childhood.

It was Doris.

Tino's sister.

My little friend from the neighborhood, from those distant days in Santo Domingo,

when we used to play in the street with rocks, laughter,

and innocence still clinging to our skin.

We hugged as if time had never passed.

She couldn't believe it was me—

the same girl who once shared snacks and secrets with her in the yard.

That reunion was a gift.

Another reminder that, even though life takes unpredictable turns,

God preserves every detail.

Even the hugs left unfinished in childhood.

And so, between prayer, work, study, and reunions,

I began to rebuild more than just a life:

I began to rebuild my faith in people... and in myself.

A Friend for the Soul

After so many nights without a blanket,

of cold trains and borrowed rooms,

of shouts, betrayals, and silences that hurt more than blows...

God gave me a friend.

Not just an acquaintance.

MY IMPACTFUL LIFE: FROM PAIN TO PURPOSE

Not just a passing companion.

A true friend.

Doris, Tino's sister,

the same little girl who once played with me in Santo Domingo,

among stones, flowers, and made-up stories,

became my confidant,

my refuge,

my shared laughter.

From the day we reunited in church,

our bond became unbreakable.

We talked almost every day.

We told each other everything.

We went out for walks,

strolled aimlessly,

looked at store windows and daydreamed

about futures that now actually seemed possible.

With her, life regained its colors.

Gray afternoons turned golden.

Painful memories found a safe place to be spoken,

without judgment, only with love.

She listened to me without interrupting.

She hugged me without me having to ask.

And many times, she cried with me… without words.

It was as if heaven, seeing my deepest wounds,

had sent Doris as a warm bandage,

a gentle touch over a broken soul.

She didn't come to erase my past,

but to teach me to walk with it…

without it weighing me down so much.

For the first time since I arrived in the United States,

I felt accompanied here on earth—

not only by God,

but by someone tangible.

Real.

Present.

And that, for a girl marked by loneliness,

was a miracle the size of a hug.

Words That Remained

There are people who speak…

and there are others whose words choose to live in your soul.

Tino was one of those wise souls,

who didn't need to raise his voice to make the heart tremble.

His voice was calm—

like gentle waters flowing over living stone…

as if every word he spoke had been prayed for before it was born.

One ordinary afternoon,

while I was washing dishes after dinner,

he came near with that fatherly, friendly look of his.

He spoke to me with tenderness...

but his words carried the weight of eternity:

—"Nuriss, every day we live is a gift from the Lord.

No matter how dark the road may seem...

God is always present."

I froze.

With wet hands.

With my soul ignited.

With my heart trembling.

Because those weren't just nice words.

They were a heavenly confirmation.

A whisper to my soul reminding me who had been with me—

in every night without a bed,

in every train without a destination,

in every tear without comfort.

I remembered that voice in the dark cell:

—"Do not be afraid. I will bring you out of here."

And I understood.

Every day—even the grayest ones,

even the most broken ones—

had been gifts disguised as storms.

Because in each one of them,

He was there.

And now, as the breeze of hope began to blow,

Tino's words were written into my spirit.

Like a shield.

Like a melody of faith.

Like a promise the soul silently recites when everything trembles:

God is always present.

What Is My Purpose?

It was a summer afternoon,

one of those when the sun warms not only the skin

but also the soul.

I was helping Ruthy with the house chores.

We swept, we dusted, and between laughter and more laughter,

the house filled with more than just cleanliness…

it filled with trust.

The open windows let in the scent of the trees

and the distant murmur of the city.

The radio played softly, with a gentle hymn in the background.

Everything seemed calm…

until she, with that sweetness only soul-mothers know how to carry,

asked me a question that disarmed me from within:

—Nuriss, sometimes life takes us down paths we never

expected,

but God always has a purpose.

Have you discovered yours here in New York?

I fell silent.

Not out of fear... but because I wanted to answer with my soul.

With truth.

I looked out the window.

I saw the buildings.

The people passing by.

The cars.

The sky.

I saw my story reflected in every corner.

And then, I took a deep breath... and answered:

—I think I am here to learn, to grow...

and to provide for my family.

I don't know God's full plan,

but I am willing to follow it.

Ruthy looked at me tenderly.

She didn't say anything.

She just smiled.

A smile that said it all.

Because she knew, just like I did,

that we don't need to understand everything...

we just need to have a willing heart.

And in that instant,

in a simple house,

on an ordinary afternoon,

I discovered that purpose doesn't always arrive with noise.

Sometimes it comes in a whisper,

between brooms, soft hymns, and prayer.

And it begins with one simple decision:

to keep walking.

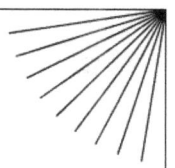

CHAPTER 9

**Facing the Pain and
Taking the First Step
The mirror of pain, moving out,
first independence**

The years passed...

like leaves falling one after another without asking permission.

And before I realized it,

the girl with the blue backpack already knew how to stand on her own.

I studied. I worked.

I got up every morning with purpose,

and little by little, what once was survival

began to look like living.

Tino and Ruthy had given me everything:

their home, their table, their affection, their time...

and most importantly: their trust.

But the day came when my wings began to feel heavier than the nest.

—Tino... Ruthy... thank you for everything.

I think it's time for me to find my own place.

I said it with a trembling voice.

Not out of fear.

Out of gratitude.

Tino, with his steady gaze, nodded.

—That means you're ready.

And though he didn't say it, I know he was proud.

Ruthy hugged me tightly,

like someone who knows her embrace is not a goodbye,

but a blessing.

That's how I began working more hours, saving,

and finally, I was able to pay the rent for my own room.

It wasn't a luxurious apartment,

nor in a fancy neighborhood,

but it was mine.

MY IMPACTFUL LIFE: FROM PAIN TO PURPOSE

A small space with a simple bed,

a window where the morning sun came in,

and a door that opened with a key—my own key.

That key represented more than a lock:

it was the entry to my new life.

That first night, I sat on the edge of the bed,

looked at the ceiling, and prayed:

—Lord, I am alone... but not alone. Thank You.

And I fell asleep in peace.

With the certainty that, after so much journey,

it was now me who began to write my own pages.

The first day I closed the door of my new room,

the echo of silence embraced me stronger than any noise of the past.

I was alone.

Truly alone.

There were no background voices,

no children's laughter,

no smell of Ruthy's home-cooked meals filling the house.

It was my space, my roof... and my challenge.

The walls were bare,

and the furniture was basic:

a simple bed, a nightstand, and a chair.

But for me, it was a palace.

I had arrived there with scars... but also with wings.

And though fear still visited me at night,

the feeling of having made it wrapped me like an invisible blanket.

The first days were difficult.

I had to learn to cook on my own —and burned more than one pot of rice—,

to manage with just enough money,

to wash my clothes, to organize myself...

and, above all, to sleep without anyone else at home.

MY IMPACTFUL LIFE: FROM PAIN TO PURPOSE

Sometimes I cried.

Other times I laughed to myself.

And many times, I prayed out loud, just to hear my own faith telling me:

—You're doing well.

My room was small,

but my gratitude was immense.

I remember looking out the window each morning and saying to the Lord:

—Thank You for this new day.

Even if I don't deserve it, here I am. Guide me.

And somehow,

each day arrived with an answer, a provision, a small victory.

Living alone wasn't easy, but it was freeing.

Because for the first time,

I wasn't in someone else's house,

nor in train stations,

nor in dark churches searching for shelter.

I was in my own little piece of the world.

And though it was tiny,

it carried the dignity of a life

that God was rebuilding with love.

The Mirror of Pain

I remember that stage clearly.

The nights felt longer.

And the days, though filled with work, carried a silence that hurt.

There were moments when, without thinking, I would stop in front of the mirror.

And there I was...

A version of myself I didn't know whether to recognize or console.

I couldn't hold my own gaze.

Not because I didn't like what I saw...

MY IMPACTFUL LIFE: FROM PAIN TO PURPOSE

but because what I felt inside was too deep.

Every time I looked at myself,

tears flowed without permission.

As if my soul whispered:

I miss you, Mom... I miss you, Dad... I need you.

It was a soft, silent cry,

born not only from physical absence,

but from everything a child should never have to carry alone.

Sometimes I spoke to the mirror.

Other times, I just lowered my head.

There were no words that could fill the void.

And yet, I stayed there...

because I knew that even though it hurt, healing was also happening.

That sadness wasn't weakness.

It was humanity.

And in the middle of the tears,

in those moments when the room became a sanctuary of sorrow,

I felt God embracing me.

Without saying a word.

Just being there.

The mirror showed me a young girl with dark circles,

with red eyes,

but with a flame that refused to go out:

a survivor.

A daughter who kept moving forward,

even when her heart was breaking into a thousand pieces.

The Quietest Christmas

Weeks turned into months.

And my life in Brooklyn, in the Richmond area, filled with new routines, hard work, cold days, and long nights.

MY IMPACTFUL LIFE: FROM PAIN TO PURPOSE

But then December came.

And with it... a sadness I couldn't explain.

The streets sparkled with colorful lights.

Stores displayed decorated trees in their windows and families smiling.

Christmas music played on every corner,

but for me, it was only noise.

There were no gifts.

No hugs.

No dinner.

No one.

It was my first Christmas completely alone.

I remember looking out the window that night,

watching the snow fall in silence,

and feeling that the silence outside

was the same silence I carried within.

I didn't turn on any lights.

I didn't make dinner.

I just sat on my bed, legs crossed,

and I cried.

I cried for my mother.

For my father.

For my brothers.

For the years that had gone by.

For the little girl who once dreamed of a different life.

And when the clock struck midnight,

I hugged my pillow and, in a soft voice, I prayed:

—"Merry Christmas, Lord... even if my heart is broken."

Days later, New Year's Eve arrived.

The world celebrated.

Fireworks lit up the sky.

Neighbors laughed, toasted, danced...

and I was once again alone.

MY IMPACTFUL LIFE: FROM PAIN TO PURPOSE

I didn't have the strength to pretend joy.

I covered myself with a sheet,

as if that could protect me from the emptiness...

and I said goodbye to the year in complete silence.

No party.

No hugs.

Only with God.

And although it hurt deeply,

I knew He was watching it all.

That He counted every tear,

that He understood every sigh...

and that this dark night

was also part of my story.

A story that, though broken,

kept moving forward.

Because my hope did not depend on the calendar...

but on a God who never left me.

Lights in the Rain

It was a rainy night.

One of those nights when the sky cries,

and you no longer need to.

I sat by the window of the room that now—yes—

I could finally call home.

The rain softly tapped against the glass,

and beyond the fogged windowpane,

the city lights flickered like tired stars.

Brooklyn was still the same: noisy, rushed, chaotic...

but I was no longer the same.

I had been transformed.

Not by luck,

but by faith.

The city that once received me with cold trains and closed doors,

now shone for me like a living promise.

A sign that yes, miracles do happen…

only sometimes they arrive disguised as struggles.

And there, with my forehead resting against the glass

and my heart beating in calm,

I began to give thanks.

Thanks for Tino and Ruthy,

for being my pillars when everything was falling apart.

Thanks for Doris, the friend who gave me laughter back.

Thanks for every church, every prayer, every borrowed bed…

and even for the cold trains,

because God was there too.

"Thank You, Lord," I cried.

"For never letting me go.

For not allowing pain to extinguish me.

For transforming me through the fire."

And as the rain kept falling,

I realized something beautiful:

I didn't just survive.

I bloomed.

In the city made of steel and concrete,

my heart—fragile and strong at the same time—

had become a silent beacon.

And on that starless night,

God reminded me that I, too, shone.

With that certainty,

with that unexplainable peace,

I sank into a restful sleep.

There was no fear anymore.

MY IMPACTFUL LIFE: FROM PAIN TO PURPOSE

No noise in my soul.

Only the soft melody of a renewed hope.

Because I understood that no matter

how harsh the journey had been,

or how heavy the rain had fallen over my story…

God was still writing.

And the best part had yet to be revealed.

I pulled the blanket over me, closed my eyes,

and while the murmur of the rain blended with my quiet breath, I said:

—"Tomorrow will be another day."

And I slept in peace,

like a warrior who finally understands

that purpose never stops…

it only moves forward.

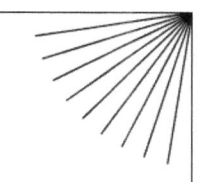

CHAPTER 10

Agustín and the Promise of Home

Several years had passed since those nights on cold trains,

since the days when I stood begging for coins in front of a payphone.

My life now had a rhythm, a stability that had cost me tears,

but tasted like victory.

That was when I received a letter from Santo Domingo.

My mother, with her sweet and excited voice, told me:

—"Nuriss, your cousin Agustín is going to New York. He's looking for an apartment, and maybe you two can share a roof."

The idea filled me with emotion.

I didn't know Agustín personally,

but the possibility of having someone of my own blood nearby,

in the middle of this immense and sometimes impersonal city…

brought me hope.

I imagined family dinners, conversations about our hometown,

and the warmth of feeling "at home," even so far away from it.

The day of his arrival, I waited with expectation.

We greeted each other politely,

with that nervous affection of two people who share a last name,

but not a history.

At first, everything seemed fine.

The first days were peaceful.

We talked. We laughed.

We shared family anecdotes,

and little by little, I began to believe that this new stage

could truly be something good.

But soon…

too soon, the signs began to show.

MY IMPACTFUL LIFE: FROM PAIN TO PURPOSE

Small things at first.

Mood swings.

Attitudes I didn't understand.

Words with a double edge.

A tension that seeped into the air without permission,

as if something wasn't right… even if I couldn't name it yet.

And that's when I realized:

not all blood guarantees safety.

Not every bond ensures protection.

The chapter with Agustín was only beginning,

and I, without knowing it,

was about to face a different storm…

one that came from within.

Agustín took me to live with him,

to what he called "our apartment"…

but what I found was nothing like what had been promised.

NURISS CLARK

Just a room.

Inside an old house.

Located on 53rd Street and Second Avenue,

in the heart of Sunset Park, Brooklyn,

very close to Bay Ridge—the area where I had once found shelter in prayer.

It was a small studio,

more like a corner walled off with partitions,

far from the "decent apartment" my mother had heard about.

Still, I told myself:

"It doesn't matter, as long as we're okay... as long as there's respect and we can move forward."

But the balance didn't last long.

I worked every single day.

Eight hours, sometimes more.

I left early, returned late,

with swollen feet and an aching back,

but with the hope that all that effort would build something better.

He didn't work.

He didn't look for work.

He had no intention of working.

The burden of rent, food, cleaning…

everything fell on me.

I was the one who filled the fridge.

The one who paid the rent.

The one who lit the stove so there would be something warm on the table.

And though at first I did it out of family love,

out of obedience,

out of that instinct to care for my own…

soon I began to realize something painful:

He wasn't here to build.

He was only here to take.

And I, naïve and not knowing what else to do,

found myself holding someone else up…

while no one was holding me.

But there was something Agustín didn't know:

I was no longer the same girl as before.

No longer the one who cried herself to sleep.

I now knew how to read the signs.

And although I wasn't yet sure how it would all end,

deep inside I already knew:

this story with him had no good path.

The Night I Had to Run

Time passed,

and what had seemed like a family refuge

slowly began turning into an invisible cell.

Agustín…

that cousin who arrived with promises and smiles,

began to reveal little by little what he had truly brought with him:

abuse disguised as closeness.

He no longer hid behind polite gestures.

His words grew harsher.

His gaze, darker.

And his presence…

more suffocating.

He didn't want a cousin.

He wanted to take advantage of a young girl alone in a foreign country.

I noticed it in the way he looked at me,

in how he stood too close,

in the comments he tossed out as if they were jokes…

but they weren't.

Until one night…

everything changed.

It was late.

Rain fell outside, as if the sky itself wanted to warn me.

Agustín walked into the room with a look in his eyes

that made my skin crawl.

And before he even said a word,

I understood everything.

He wanted to force me.

He wanted to steal what didn't belong to him.

He wanted to hurt me.

My heart leapt out of my chest.

My soul screamed: **Run!**

And that's what I did.

I ran.

I ran as if hell itself were chasing me.

I ran without knowing where I was going,

only knowing I couldn't stay another second.

I burst out into the street under the rain.

Barefoot.

Soaked.

Shivering from the cold... and from fear.

But alive.

With every step I took,

I felt God whisper:

—"I am with you.

I will not let you fall."

I didn't look back.

I didn't stop.

I ran until my body could no longer move...

but my spirit never gave in.

That night wasn't just an escape.

It was a liberation.

It was God's voice pulling me out from the wolf disguised as kin.

It was my soul declaring: **"You will not destroy me here!"**

And though my body was exhausted,

and the rain embraced me with its sadness,

I knew, through my sobs,

that this was not a night of defeat...

it was a night of courage.

Days went by.

And with each sunrise, my soul healed a little more.

The fear remained, like a shadow.

But I also held the certainty that I had not been born to live in fear.

I was not going to stay silent.

I was not going to keep being a victim.

I was no longer that defenseless girl.

Now, I had a voice. And I was going to use it.

With trembling legs, yes—

but with fire in my heart—

I confronted Agustín.

I looked him in the eyes, not lowering my head this time, and I said:

—"If you ever come near me again with dirty intentions, I will call the police.

And this time, I won't run... this time, you'll face the law."

He said nothing.

Cowardice stole his words.

He gathered his things, and he left.

He left with the same shadow he had brought with him.

And for the first time in a long while...

I breathed.

The room felt different.

It was no longer a place of fear.

It was my space.

My territory, reclaimed.

I kept living there, alone.

But not like before.

Now, the silence didn't oppress me.

It protected me.

Now, the walls were no longer witnesses of danger...

they were witnesses of my strength.

I looked at myself in the mirror again.

And this time, I didn't cry.

I smiled.

Because I saw a woman who had not been broken.

And I understood that...

sometimes, raising your voice

is the first step toward lifting your soul again.

Rebuilding My Life

After Agustín left,

the air changed.

It was as if the room breathed with me,

as if the walls no longer held secrets but freedom.

Being alone again,

after so much,

didn't come without fear... but it came with strength.

Little by little, I began to rebuild myself.

I cleaned not only my surroundings,

but also my inner self.

I removed things I didn't need.

I moved the bed to a different corner.

I opened the window more often.

And I started writing thoughts in an old notebook...

a way to remind my soul that it was safe.

NURISS CLARK

I looked for work.

I went back to school at night.

And with each step, though small,

I felt myself being reborn.

I no longer depended on anyone.

Only on God... and on my determination.

I came home late from work,

but no longer with sadness,

instead with the dignified exhaustion

of someone rising with dignity.

I began surrounding myself with new people,

healthy, genuine, good people.

Life started to reward me with souls who didn't hurt me,

but who lifted me up.

On Sundays, I returned to church,

to sing with different tears...

MY IMPACTFUL LIFE: FROM PAIN TO PURPOSE

not of pain, but of gratitude.

My faith, far from fading, became deeper.

More real. More alive.

I looked back with respect,

not torment.

I knew I couldn't change what I had lived through,

but I could choose what to build from it.

And that's what I did.

Day by day.

With trembling, yet steady steps.

With a heart still wounded,

but determined.

And one day, without even noticing…

I stopped surviving. And I began living.

I lived in a neighborhood where smoke filled the air.

But it wasn't incense,

nor the steam of a hot meal...

it was marijuana. Drugs.

Despair disguised as fun.

The young people around me were immersed in a dark world,

one that for them was routine... and for me, a warning.

Their laughter was forced.

Their conversations always broken,

as if their thoughts no longer belonged to them.

I didn't fit in. Nor did I want to.

I remember looking out the window and seeing them gathered,

smoking on the corners,

passing little bags from hand to hand...

and I, in silence, prayed—asking the Lord to keep me firm, set apart.

In the midst of that clouded environment,

there was a light that guided me every week:

Emmanuel Church.

It was located on 55th Street, not far from where I lived.

And even though the neighborhood sometimes felt more like a trap than a home,

my walk to the temple was my escape.

My appointment with God's presence.

I walked alone, but I never felt alone.

The Lord walked with me. Step by step. Street by street.

The church was small,

but as soon as I crossed its doors, I felt a peace I couldn't find anywhere else.

There, there was no smoke—

there was praise.

There was no noise—

there was direction.

At every service, the Lord ministered to me and said:

Do not be contaminated.

Do not stop.

You were set apart.

While many were being lost,

I was being found.

While many were falling,

I was holding on.

And even though I was young,

even though I was alone,

even though temptation lingered on every corner...

I knew who I was.

I knew who I belonged to.

I knew my life would not end on a corner smoking...

but on high ground, proclaiming.

Immersed in His Presence

It was a different kind of Sunday,

a day the heavens had already written into its pages.

Emmanuel Church, there on 55th Street,

was alive with a gentle fire,

as if the angels were already taking their places.

There was an air of expectation—

the kind you feel when God has something prepared.

That day, I wasn't just going to church as usual…

I was going to surrender completely.

I was going to be baptized.

I was going to die…

to be born again.

It wasn't a death of the body,

but of wounds, fears, and broken pasts…

and the birth of something new, pure, strong.

A soul washed, sealed, and set apart for God.

I didn't know if I had the words to express what I was feeling...

but my spirit was already saying it all:

Here I am, Lord. All Yours.

The temple filled with songs,

and I felt heaven listening.

The worship seemed to touch invisible strings within me,

and every word from the altar fell as confirmation.

When they called me to the front,

my legs trembled.

It was an eternal step—

a covenant sealed in water,

but written in heavenly fire.

My hands shook.

My soul burned.

A force overcame me.

I felt fire in my bones.

I cried.

I trembled.

I broke…

but not in sadness—

in surrender.

The congregation sang,

the pastor prayed,

and I…

I was being reborn.

That was the day God told me:

"You are Mine.

And from this day on, you walk in authority."

And then something happened that I will never forget:

The floor of the altar began to open.

As if a secret had been hidden beneath the ground,

a pool emerged from the depths of the floor.

A baptismal font that wasn't always visible,

but revealed only for holy moments—

as if heaven itself descended in the form of water.

It was small, discreet,

but within it was the glory of the living God.

I stepped in, my heart pounding like a drum of war and worship.

There was no turning back.

This was my moment.

They immersed me.

The water wrapped around me like a mantle.

And as I sank beneath it,

I felt everything old fall away.

Everything dirty, everything broken,

everything that had once hurt me…

was left behind in those waters.

MY IMPACTFUL LIFE: FROM PAIN TO PURPOSE

And when I rose,

I rose different.

Not just wet,

but anointed.

The church applauded.

The congregation wept.

And I...

I simply felt heaven within me.

The place,

the people,

the moment...

all had been prepared with purpose.

That hidden pool...

reminded me that sometimes the most sacred things are the ones others cannot see.

And that what God has reserved for you,

neither life, nor the enemy, nor pain can ever take away.

I left that place bathed in glory.

Sealed in fire.

And from that day on...

I was never the same.

After that day,

something within me changed forever.

It was no longer just about surviving.

Now I walked with the awareness that I had been sealed, set apart, chosen.

Yes, my routine continued—

work, house chores, the same trains, the same streets of Brooklyn...

but I was no longer the same woman walking them.

Fear no longer had the same hold on me.

The past no longer carried the same weight.

And loneliness... that old shadow, could no longer touch me.

Every morning I rose with a prayer on my lips,

and with a strength that didn't come from me,

but from the One who had lifted me from the water to set me ablaze with fire.

I returned to Emmanuel Church with greater commitment.

I joined the weekly meetings, the prayer services.

I began to serve wherever I could—

even if it was just arranging chairs or helping with the youth.

Something within me longed for more.

More of His presence.

More of His will.

More of His voice.

And it wasn't long before it happened...

One night, during a prayer vigil,

the Spirit of God poured out with indescribable power.

Hands were lifted high.

Hearts were broken open.

And I...

I was filled.

Filled like a cup overflowing with oil.

I began to speak in tongues,

my knees trembled, and I fell before the altar.

It was fire.

Not literal, but heavenly fire.

A fire that consumed me from within,

burning away doubts, traumas, wounds.

That night I understood something:

the baptism of water had washed me...

but the baptism of fire had activated me.

I was no longer just a survivor.

Now, I was a carrier of light.

And with each passing day,

the desire to help, to serve, to share my story...

grew like a seed watered by the tears of my prayers.

The past no longer defined me.

Now, I used it as a platform.

And from that moment, I knew:

Everything I had lived through had not been in vain.

God was preparing me for something greater.

And I was only just beginning.

Between Books and Purpose

Brooklyn College was not just a university for me.

It was an altar. A battlefield.

A platform of destiny.

While others went to class with light backpacks,

I carried more than books...

I carried history.

I carried scars.

I carried God's promises yet to be fulfilled.

And still, I walked with my head held high.

Not because I thought I was better,

but because I knew the price I had paid to get there.

In addition to studying,

I found a job on campus through a program called *Work-Study*.

I worked in administrative offices,

filing papers, organizing materials, answering phone calls.

It wasn't glamorous, but it was provision.

It was dignity.

It was opportunity.

It was a seed I knew would one day bear fruit.

I went from class straight to work.

And sometimes, afterward, I would go to serve at church.

I slept little. But I lived with purpose.

MY IMPACTFUL LIFE: FROM PAIN TO PURPOSE

I remember looking out the window of the office where I worked

and watching students rushing back and forth.

Some complained about assignments.

Others didn't value what they had.

And I... I simply smiled,

because I knew that being there was no accident.

It was fulfillment. It was redemption.

It was God saying to me:

"I keep My promises."

As I filed documents,

I was also filing away dreams.

As I organized reports,

I was also organizing my future.

I didn't have luxuries.

Sometimes I didn't even have enough to buy a coffee between classes.

But what I did have

was a fire in my soul that no obstacle could extinguish.

And it was there, between folders and notebooks,

that God spoke to me:

"You are planted in fertile ground, daughter.

Keep growing.

Keep bearing fruit.

Your story is only beginning."

CHAPTER 11

Driving Towards Purpose
My Work as a Taxi Driver

The classroom shaped me.

The church strengthened me.

But the real world... the real world pushed me to make bold decisions.

That was when the opportunity came.

A friend of my sister Lourdes, moved by my story, decided to lend me $5,000.

—"For you to buy a car and a radio, Nuriss.

You can do this. Go after your dream."

His faith ignited something inside me.

And even though it was a risky investment...

I didn't hesitate.

I knew that working as a taxi driver in New York was no easy task.

Even less for a woman.

Even less for a young woman.

Even less for someone who was still studying and carrying so much pain.

But that was exactly the fuel that propelled me.

With those $5,000, I bought a modest car,

and a radio to communicate with the dispatch base,

as was customary at the time.

No apps. No advanced technology.

Just a radio, a voice in my ear,

and the courage to say:

"I'm ready for the next call."

By day, I was a student.

By night, I became the taxi driver who broke barriers.

And indeed, I did.

Many customers were surprised to see me.

Some stared.

Others laughed with admiration:

MY IMPACTFUL LIFE: FROM PAIN TO PURPOSE

—"A woman taxi driver? Where has that been seen?"

—"Here. With me.

Now sit tight, I'll get you there safely."

The tips were good,

but even better was the feeling of taking the wheel of my own life.

I drove through streets, avenues, alleys, highways…

each route a story.

Each passenger, a lesson.

Each night, a victory.

Sometimes I left work with aching feet,

with my hands tense from gripping the steering wheel,

with eyes half-shut from exhaustion.

But I looked at myself in the mirror and said:

—"Nuriss, you're making it.

You're writing history."

And it wasn't just about the money,

nor the car,

nor the radio.

It was because every time I started the engine...

I felt as if heaven itself whispered:

"Keep driving, daughter.

Your destination lies ahead.

And you are reaching it."

Being a taxi driver was more than driving.

It was like being guided by a divine frequency,

even when all I heard was the static of the radio.

One cold night,

the streets of New York shimmered with the reflections of traffic lights and the weary thoughts of the city.

I was vehicle 71,

and my shift was almost over.

—"Base to vehicle 71. There's a call on 112th and Lexington. Do you take it?"

MY IMPACTFUL LIFE: FROM PAIN TO PURPOSE

I grabbed the microphone quickly:

—"This is 71. On my way."

I drove to the location.

The silence of the city seemed to ride with me.

But my heart was pounding...

as if something special was about to happen.

A middle-aged man got into the back seat.

Well dressed, composed, but with a gaze

that revealed many internal battles.

—"To 5th Avenue, please."

—"Of course," I replied, focusing on the road.

During the ride, we barely spoke.

Only the murmur of the city and the sound of his tired breathing.

The meter marked $7.

But the lesson he carried... was priceless.

He reached into his coat,

pulled out his wallet,

and began to count.

One.

Two.

Three...

Three hundred dollars!

He handed it to me without hesitation,

with a smile full of genuine gratitude.

—"This is for you.

For your effort, for your respect,

and because not everyone has your courage."

And without waiting for a reply, he stepped out of the car

and disappeared among the buildings of the great city.

I was frozen.

A $300 tip...

for a $7 fare.

MY IMPACTFUL LIFE: FROM PAIN TO PURPOSE

My eyes filled with tears.

I gripped the wheel tightly.

And in a whisper, through sobs of gratitude, I said to God:

—"Thank You.

Thank You, because I know it was You.

You always provide. You always surprise."

That night I understood that, even if the world doesn't see you,

even if your effort seems invisible...

God is keeping record.

And when He rewards,

He does it His way...

and with heavenly interest.

From that night on, after receiving $300 for a $7 ride,

something inside me ignited.

I no longer just expected passengers...

I expected miracles.

And they came.

Again and again.

Day after day,

I met completely different people,

but all with one common gesture:

they looked at me...

and something in their faces changed.

It was as if they saw in me

not just a driver...

but a story. A struggle.

A brave soul.

And then... they blessed me.

I remember one afternoon I was dispatched to pick someone up for a ride to JFK Airport.

Traffic was heavy,

the city was boiling with movement,

and I prayed silently within myself:

MY IMPACTFUL LIFE: FROM PAIN TO PURPOSE

—"Lord, if You are with me, show me that I am not alone."

The passenger was an older man,

very kind, soft-spoken, with tired eyes and wisdom in his voice.

We spoke little, but something touched him.

Something moved his heart.

When we reached the airport, the meter read exactly $40.

I reached out my hand to collect the fare,

and then... it happened.

He handed me a stack of bills.

$500! And he said:

—"For you, young lady.

Because something in you tells me you need it.

And because the world needs more women like you."

I couldn't speak.

I just cried.

I cried and cried,

with the money in my hands and my heart lifted to heaven.

Every night I returned home with a full soul.

Not just because of the tips.

But because I knew God was using me,

testing me,

and showing me that even in the most unexpected job,

He can shine.

And He did.

Through me.

Seeds of Abundance

The days went by...

the rides went by...

the passengers came and went,

and with them, the miracles continued.

Every dollar that came into my hands was not just money:

MY IMPACTFUL LIFE: FROM PAIN TO PURPOSE

it was a seed.

And like every good sower,

I didn't just collect...

I saved.

I planted in myself. In my future. In my freedom.

With every unexpected tip,

with every night I came home exhausted but overflowing with gratitude,

my bank account—the very same one that had once been empty—

began to grow.

And while all the other drivers—men, every single one of them—

watched me arrive at the base with determination,

they didn't know they were witnessing the story of a pioneer.

—"How do you manage to drive so many hours all alone?"

—"Aren't you afraid of being out there at night?"

—"And how do you always get such good tips?"

I just smiled.

They could never understand that there was a grace upon me—

a grace that could not be explained.

A woman alone, yes…

but backed by heaven.

My goal was clear:

save. Invest. Move forward.

And then the moment I had been waiting for arrived…

to pay my debt.

To honor the one who believed in me.

His name was Leo.

A friend of my sister Lourdes.

A man who didn't know me well,

but who believed in me when I needed it most.

MY IMPACTFUL LIFE: FROM PAIN TO PURPOSE

He had lent me $5,000 to buy my first car and the radio that connected me to the base.

And thanks to that gesture…

everything began.

With every tip saved,

with every dollar set aside with discipline,

I gathered what I needed.

And one day, with my heart overflowing with emotion,

I called him and said:

—"Leo, here it is.

Every cent you lent me.

And with it, my eternal gratitude."

He smiled.

I cried.

And we both knew that this transaction was not merely financial…

it was spiritual.

It was redemptive.

It was part of the story of a woman who never gave up.

To this day,

I thank Leo deeply.

Because without knowing it,

he was a key piece in God's plan for my life.

Bricks of Purpose

I had worked hard.

I had cried, prayed, driven, and endured.

Now… the time had come to build.

I was no longer borrowing.

Now I was investing.

With the savings I had gathered as a taxi driver,

with God's backing and the experience life had given me,

I made a bold decision:

MY IMPACTFUL LIFE: FROM PAIN TO PURPOSE

to open my own office.

The first one was on 57th Street and 4th Avenue in Brooklyn.

A small but powerful office that began as a travel agency and public notary.

I decorated that place with my own hands,

placing every detail as if I were raising an embassy of heaven.

Because that's what it was to me:

a living testimony of what God can do with a surrendered life.

People came from everywhere seeking help:

tickets, paperwork, letters, advice.

And I was there to serve.

But something inside me whispered there was still more…

something that pushed me to look higher.

And then it happened.

I took another step.

I opened a second office.

This time, on 54th Street... and this one was different.

This was for Real Estate.

My professional career had been born!

I had gone from sleeping in trains to helping others find their homes.

From having no roof of my own, to selling roofs for entire families.

From not knowing what I would eat...

to signing contracts with clients who trusted me.

It was official:

I, Nuriss, was a broker.

And my story was only just beginning.

I looked at my offices with shining eyes and a heart that trembled with joy.

I remembered every sacrifice, every tear, every freezing night...

and I understood that it had all been worth it.

Because where others saw just a door...

I saw a mission.

Every client was a life.

Every property, a seed of the future.

Every signature, a celebration in heaven.

The First Big Closing

The papers were ready.

The contract was on the table.

The ink still fresh.

My heart pounded like a war drum...

but not out of fear,

out of victory.

After so much effort, after sleepless nights,

after days walking streets, visiting properties, talking to people,

the moment had finally arrived.

My first big closing.

The client looked me in the eyes and signed.

His trust was absolute.

I had shown him the way with transparency, dedication, and faith.

And now... the sale was sealed.

The commission was $25,000.

Twenty-five thousand dollars!

I had never held that amount in my hands before, ever.

It felt like the whole of heaven was celebrating with me.

And it wasn't just about the money.

It was about everything it represented.

It represented every tear hidden inside a train car.

Every prayer whispered through trembling lips.

Every long shift driving taxis, every night I spent not knowing what would become of me.

And now...

here I was.

MY IMPACTFUL LIFE: FROM PAIN TO PURPOSE

Signing contracts.

Owning my business.

Writing a new story with every stroke of the pen.

When I walked out of that office with the check in my hand,

I cried.

I cried with a sob that came from the depths of my being.

A cry of gratitude, of fulfillment, of awe.

"Lord," I said, looking up to the sky,

"Thank You. Thank You for never letting me go.

Thank You for believing in me when no one else did.

Thank You for not letting me give up."

That was only the beginning.

From that day forward, my confidence soared.

I knew I was not improvising.

I knew I was exactly where I was meant to be.

The girl who once asked for five cents at a train station

was now signing checks worth thousands at a closing table.

And deep within me, I knew…

that check was only the first.

Because when God opens a door,

the flow doesn't stop.

It only grows.

From Clients to Homeowners

My office was alive.

The sound of computer keys tapping, the hum of the printer, the murmur of conversations,

the aroma of coffee in the mornings,

and above all, the atmosphere of purpose that filled every transaction and every consultation.

I had a travel agency.

I offered notary services, accounting, and tax preparation.

And with time, something extraordinary began to happen…

MY IMPACTFUL LIFE: FROM PAIN TO PURPOSE

The same clients who came to file their taxes,

who bought a plane ticket,

or who needed to send money...

also began to hear me speak to them about a greater dream.

—"Are you still paying rent?" I would ask with that confident smile that had become my signature.

—"Did you know that with that same money, you can own your home?"

—"I'll help you. I'll explain it step by step. Look, if you can pay $1,800 in rent, you can pay a mortgage. You can be a homeowner!"

And that's how I planted the first seed.

One by one, they began to take interest.

People who never imagined owning anything...

began to dream.

And more than that: they began to act.

I explained everything to them: how credit worked,

how to qualify,

what steps were needed in the process,

what it took to get a loan,

how to prepare their documents...

I educated them.

And that turned me not just into a broker, but into a guide.

My portfolio of clients was born!

And it wasn't because I went looking for them...

It was because I served them.

Each story was different.

A mechanic. A nurse. A single mother. A newcomer.

All with a common need:

someone who believed in them.

And I, who once didn't even have a roof of my own...

became the woman handing them the keys to their very first home.

That's how this unstoppable flow of clients began.

Not through advertising.

But through living testimony. Through transformation.

Because where others saw only numbers,

I saw families.

I saw stories.

I saw dreams that deserved to become reality.

CHAPTER 12

The Key to a Dream

The sun streamed through the corners of Sixth Avenue in Brooklyn.

That day seemed brighter, as if even the sky knew

that something sacred was about to happen.

In my hand, I held a silver keychain.

It gleamed like a promise fulfilled.

It was the first key I would ever hand over in my career...

and not just to anyone.

But to **Aurora Sánchez**.

Aurora was a fighter.

A mother. A dreamer.

She had lived her whole life believing that owning a home

was a luxury for others, but not for her.

—"I never thought I could be the owner of a house here in New York,"

she told me the first time we sat down to talk about real estate.

And I looked at her with faith in my eyes and replied:

—"Aurora, of course you can. The only thing you need is to believe it...

and I'll help you with the rest."

I guided her step by step.

Credit. Pre-qualification. Documents. Inspection. Closing.

And now, here we were, standing in front of her home...

a home she had once dreamed of,

but had never dared to imagine so close.

—"Are you ready?" I asked, as I held out the key.

Aurora trembled.

Her eyes sparkled with restrained emotion.

—"Is this real?" she whispered.

—"This house... is mine?"

MY IMPACTFUL LIFE: FROM PAIN TO PURPOSE

When her fingers touched the keychain,

a silent tear rolled down her cheek.

And in that moment, I cried too.

I walked her to the door.

She opened it with trembling hands...

and took her first step as a homeowner.

The walls seemed to welcome her with open arms.

The empty rooms were already filled with promises.

The silence of the house spoke of hope.

—"Here... here I will rest.

Here I will build a new beginning,"

Aurora said, her voice breaking but full of determination.

I stood for a few seconds on the sidewalk,

watching her walk through her new home.

And in my heart, something clicked.

I wasn't just handing over keys.

I was unlocking destinies.

I was answering a call greater than myself.

From that day forward, I knew that every property sold was a collective victory.

A shared triumph between God, human effort...

and a little piece of me.

A Voice That Ignited the Dream

"Why rent when you can own?"

That question wasn't just a sales pitch.

It was a calling.

It was an awakening.

People came to my office to file their taxes,

buy a plane ticket, sign a power of attorney...

and they left with a seed of hope planted in their hearts.

The word began to spread.

First one.

MY IMPACTFUL LIFE: FROM PAIN TO PURPOSE

Then five.

Then dozens.

My office was filling up.

My schedule was overflowing.

And my phone lines wouldn't stop ringing.

—"You're the woman who helps people buy houses, right?"

—"I want you to help me too."

—"My cousin told me about you."

—"My neighbor said that thanks to you, she's now a homeowner."

And just like that, a movement was born.

People who never thought they could own property

began to believe that it was possible.

My voice, my conviction, my experience...

became tools of liberation.

It was as if God was using my story—

the girl who once had nowhere to sleep—

to now remind the world that yes, it can be done.

Yes, there is a way.

Yes, there is an open door.

And the most beautiful part was that I didn't have to convince anyone.

The results spoke for me.

The keys handed over.

The families celebrating.

The contracts signed with tears in their eyes.

"Why rent when you can own?"

It was more than a phrase.

It was my banner.

My testimony.

My battle won.

When my office began to flourish and clients kept coming,

I understood something very clearly:

MY IMPACTFUL LIFE: FROM PAIN TO PURPOSE

the purpose wasn't just to sell houses...

it was to lift others up so they too could transform lives.

And so my mission multiplied.

Not only was I helping people buy homes,

I also began training agents, mentoring them, inspiring them.

Giving them the tools I never had.

I taught them everything:

how to talk to clients,

how to listen to their needs,

how to understand the market,

how to walk with faith and dignity through every closing.

It wasn't just technical training...

it was training with purpose.

And soon, the office was full of names that still echo in my memory with pride:

Nilva, with her sweet laughter and servant's heart.

Toribio, always ready to run out and show a property at the last minute.

Santo, serene and patient, but with an inner strength that inspired respect.

Rosa, determined and steadfast like an oak that doesn't bend in the wind.

Buzina, charismatic, with an energy that drew every client in.

Milly, meticulous, passionate, and detail-oriented in every transaction.

Daisy, who became an expert at helping large families find their ideal home.

Johanny, a warrior in heels, who learned fast and soared high.

And many, many more.

Each one came with their story,

with their struggles, with their fears...

but also with a hunger to learn.

And with me, they learned to serve, to shine, to close with integrity.

MY IMPACTFUL LIFE: FROM PAIN TO PURPOSE

I sat with them like a mother with her children,

sharing not only my techniques,

but also my scars.

Because I wanted them to know that yes, it's possible—

but you have to fight for every dream.

And when I saw one of them hand over their first key,

or receive their first commission check,

I felt as if I were witnessing the harvest of my sleepless nights.

From being a woman alone with a taxi...

I now had a team of agents,

of leaders,

of miracle-workers on earth.

Because every property closed by one of them

was also a victory of mine...

and of the Kingdom.

NURISS CLARK

My First Home, My Own Key

I had helped so many people find their homes...

I had handed over keys, shared hugs,

and witnessed tears of joy in hundreds of clients.

But this time, the key was for me.

After years of effort, work, learning, and struggle,

the time finally came to sign my own deed.

The property was in Queens.

A neighborhood full of life, history, and soul.

The streets welcomed me as if they knew

that I wasn't just another buyer...

but a survivor who had finally reached her promise.

I walked through the door with the key trembling in my hand.

It wasn't just a house...

it was the confirmation that everything I had lived through...

MY IMPACTFUL LIFE: FROM PAIN TO PURPOSE

was not in vain.

The walls seemed to embrace me.

The floor creaked beneath my feet as if celebrating each step.

The echo of my voice in the empty house sounded like a song of victory.

—"This house is mine!" I shouted aloud,

and then I burst into tears.

I remembered everything:

The nights on the train.

The freezing stations.

The bank. The injustices.

The silent prayers.

The closed doors.

And now... this door opened with *my* key.

I lived there for a beautiful season,

surrounded by my first plants, my first decorations,

and the peace that comes from having a place you can truly call your own.

It was a simple home,

but within its corners lived my story.

In every window, a sigh of gratitude.

In every room, a living testimony.

That house in Queens was not the end… it was the beginning.

Later, Long Island would come, new stages would unfold…

but that first property will always hold a sacred place in my soul.

Because it was there, within those walls,

that I understood God had not only given me a roof…

but also purpose,

authority,

and territory.

CHAPTER 13

Conquered Territory

After owning my first home in Queens,

something inside me began to beat with strength.

It was no longer just about living...

it was about possessing.

About leaving a legacy.

About multiplying.

And that's how the opportunities began to arrive.

As if heaven itself had aligned with my steps,

I started hearing about multifamily properties for sale.

Two-family and three-family homes.

And the most surprising part: they were within my reach.

It wasn't coincidence.

It was God's grace and favor covering me.

Guiding me.

Confirming that the time had come to step up to the next level.

My heart raced every time I walked into a property.

The walls might be worn,

the ceilings low,

the windows old...

but I didn't see ruins.

I saw future.

The first multifamily property I bought was a two-family house.

The moment I closed the deal,

something inside me broke... and lifted at the same time.

It was as if the Lord was telling me:

"I promised I would give you a home... but I will also give you territory."

After that purchase, everything began to flow.

MY IMPACTFUL LIFE: FROM PAIN TO PURPOSE

I acquired a property on Smith Street,

right in the heart of Downtown Brooklyn.

Where others only saw noise, traffic, and urban chaos,

I saw a gold mine.

A high-traffic area, perfect for investment,

with easy access to the subway, offices, restaurants, and shops.

I knew it would be a jewel over time.

And so it was.

Then, I positioned myself in Park Slope,

one of the most elegant and desired neighborhoods in Brooklyn.

Tree-lined streets reaching up to the sky,

quiet blocks with historic architecture,

young families, professionals, artists...

and now also: me.

And as if that weren't enough,

the Lord led me to Fifth Avenue in Brooklyn.

A strategic, vibrant area, full of movement.

There, too, I left my mark,

adding yet another property to my blessed portfolio.

Each acquisition was a declaration of faith.

That yes, it is possible—when God goes before you.

I put my stamp on every property.

I improved them, cared for them, honored them.

I wasn't just an investor—

I was a steward of God's favor.

The rentals began generating steady income.

The value of the properties rose every year.

And my name started to be recognized not only as a broker,

but also as an investor.

As a reference.

As a woman of influence.

And all of this...

began with a key.

And with a promise:

that if I trusted God,

He would give me much more than I had ever lost.

Long Island – Where the Land Became Rest

After years of sowing in Brooklyn,

building offices, handing over keys,

and expanding my portfolio of properties...

the Lord led me into a new stage.

A stage of peace.

A stage of solid ground.

Long Island. Nassau County.

It wasn't just a change of neighborhood,

it was a transition in my soul.

A gift of rest.

A fulfilled promise.

The day I walked through the door of that house,

my heart trembled.

There was something different in the air.

It was as if the whole story of my life whispered:

"Now it is time to dwell, not just survive."

The house was spacious, full of light,

with a garden that became my sanctuary.

The trees swayed with the wind,

as if they were celebrating my arrival.

And I—who once slept in trains and stations…

now had my own corner of heaven.

I lived there for years.

There I rested.

There I healed.

MY IMPACTFUL LIFE: FROM PAIN TO PURPOSE

There I regained strength.

There I cried for everything I had lived.

And I also laughed in freedom for everything I had conquered.

Each morning, the song of the birds mingled with my prayers.

The sunlight filtering through the curtains was more than natural light:

it was the reflection of God's presence telling me:

"You are in your promised land."

In that home, I discovered new things about myself.

I learned to love myself,

to enjoy the silence,

to cultivate flowers,

to drink tea in peace...

and to prepare for what was to come.

Because from that house, I began to dream bigger.

I began to plan new businesses.

To write.

To map out the next steps.

It was my base,

my nest,

my sacred refuge.

There in Long Island, my story did not stop…

it was strengthened.

It was in Nassau County where my spirit learned to rest…

and my mind prepared to keep conquering.

And every time I went out to the garden,

barefoot on the fresh grass,

I looked at the sky and said:

"Thank You, Lord.

Because You not only gave me a house…

You gave me a home.

You gave me identity.

You gave me rest.

And this land...

You also made it mine."

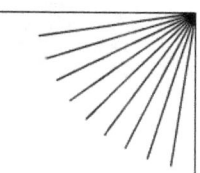

CONCLUSION

Up to Here... But Not the End

If you've made it this far, thank you.

Thank you for walking with me through cold streets,

for sitting by my side on empty trains,

for crying with my silent tears and also for celebrating my victories.

Every page of this book was written with my soul.

Every word was born from the deepest part of my memories,

from a life marked by trials...

but also by promises fulfilled.

This is not only the story of a girl who traveled alone with a heart full of dreams.

This is the story of someone who believed...

when there was no reason to.

Who resisted... when everything said no.

Who held on... when the world let go of her hand.

This is my story.

But it can also be yours.

Because if there is one thing I have learned,

it is that the same God who lifted me up,

can also lift you up.

Today I close this first edition here...

in Florida, USA,

in this home that is my rest,

my refuge, my altar.

But my story doesn't end here.

No, my dear reader.

The best is yet to be told.

There are many more pages to write,

many battles I fought,

and many more victories I achieved.

"To be continued..."

Because as long as there is breath in my chest,

I will keep sharing every part of this living testimony.

Thank you for walking with me.

Thank you for believing with me.

Thank you for reading me... and for feeling me.

With much love,

NURISS

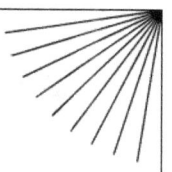

FINAL PRAYER

May This Story Awaken Your Purpose

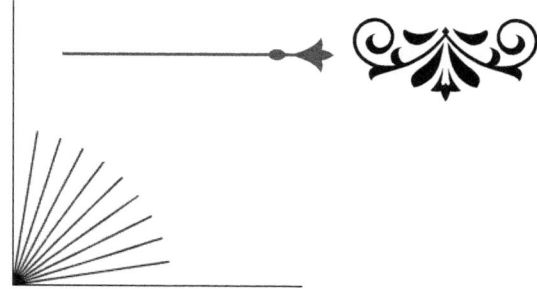

Dear God,

Thank You for every life that has reached these final pages.

You know their story, their pain, their sleepless nights, and their unanswered questions.

Today, I ask with all my heart that what they have read will not be just words on a page…

but a breath of hope, a fire that ignites the soul, a confirmation that they are not alone.

Pour out Your grace upon every reader.

Heal their wounds, open a way where there seems to be none, and strengthen their steps.

Remind them that pain does not define their destiny,

but that You, Lord, even use tears as seeds to reap glory—

where the initial struggle and sorrow are transformed into joy and abundance.

May this story not end here…

but instead awaken dormant dreams, move hearts,

and be a testimony that You are still the God of miracles.

I declare over every person holding this book:

that their life will be transformed,

that their purpose will be activated,

and that what is yet to come will be far greater than what has been left behind.

And I pray that each reader will be blessed by You, Lord.

That everything they touch will prosper.

That Your eternal promise will be fulfilled in their lives, just as it is written in Deuteronomy 28:8:

"The Lord will send a blessing on your barns and on everything you put your hand to.

The Lord your God will bless you in the land He is giving you."

May God bless you abundantly.

May this book be a seed of faith, purpose, and multiplication in your life.

In the mighty name of Jesus,

Amen.

PHOTOGRAPHS AND LETTERS FROM MY PARENTS

**Envelopes with Stamps
and Addresses showing postmarks
and my parents' handwriting**

These images and letters are treasures of my journey. Each photograph holds a memory, a moment that marked my life. Each letter from my parents was a lighthouse in the darkness, a reminder that even far away, their love was with me. I share them here so that this book is not only made of words, but also, memories, and indelible marks.

Nuriss Clark

Is a woman whose life embodies resilience, purpose, and transformation.

She graduated in Theology from **Logos Christian University** in Jacksonville, Florida, with an Associate Degree in Biblical Studies. She is also a licensed Real Estate Broker in both Florida and New York.

In her twenties, she opened her first real estate office in Brooklyn, NY. Thanks to an extraordinary volume of sales, her company was recognized by **Dunn & Bradstreet** as a new business generating millions of dollars in sales within its very first quarter.

For over 20 years, she has worked across multiple areas of real estate—residential, commercial, and industrial. She has also served as a mortgage broker, insurance agent, tax and accounting specialist, with extensive expertise in FHA, VA, conventional loans, and other financial products.

But beyond her impressive career, she is a woman who chose to turn her pain into purpose.

As a teenager, she emigrated alone to the United States with no family to receive her and only $32 in her pocket. She slept in train stations, faced hunger, abuse, and betrayal—yet she never lost her faith or her hope.

Her story is a living testimony to the power of faith, perseverance, and God's grace. From having nothing, she became a successful entrepreneur, investor, and now a motivational author committed to inspiring others never to give up.

Her book, **"My Impactful Life: From Pain to Purpose"**, is not just a story—it awakens, empowers, and uplifts.

Today, Nuriss lives with gratitude, fully committed to her calling and determined to leave a legacy of hope, strength, and faith.

www.ingramcontent.com/pod-product-compliance
Lightning Source LLC
Chambersburg PA
CBHW072000150426
43194CB00008B/938